D1457255

ENDANGERED SPECIES:
ISSUES AND ANALYSES

ENDANGERED SPECIES:
ISSUES AND ANALYSES

PAUL FOREMAN (EDITOR)

Nova Science Publishers, Inc.
New York

Senior Editors: Susan Boriotti and Donna Dennis
Coordinating Editor: Tatiana Shohov
Office Manager: Annette Hellinger
Graphics: Wanda Serrano
Book Production: Matthew Kozlowski, Jonathan Rose and Jennifer Vogt
Circulation: Raymond Davis, Cathy DeGregory and Ave Maria Gonzalez
Communications and Acquisitions: Serge P. Shohov

Library of Congress Cataloging-in-Publication Data

Foreman, Paul.
    Endangered species: issues and analyses / Paul Foreman.
      p. cm.
    ISBN 1-59033-161-3.
    1. Endangered species—Law and legislation—United States. I. Title.

KF5640 .F67 2002
346.7304'69522—dc21

2001059047

Copyright © 2002 by Nova Science Publishers, Inc.
      400 Oser Avenue, Suite 1600
      Hauppauge, New York 11788-3619
      Tele. 631-231-7269   Fax 631-231-8175
      E Mail: Novascience@earthlink.net
      www.novapublishers.com

CONTENTS

PREFACE

Protecting natural resources remains an important environmental priority in the United States. The Endangered Species Act along with its revisions, exemptions, amendments and enforcement are significant factors in this effort. This book presents the background of the Act along with analyses of developments and current issues. The focus of attention of these analyses is the Act and its consequencs, but between the lines the battle remains over profits for companies reaping the benefits of the natural resources. On the other side are the over-protectors who would protect every blade of grass from developers.

Chapter 1

THE ENDANGERED SPECIES ACT: CONSIDERATION OF ECONOMIC FACTORS

Pamela Baldwin

INTRODUCTION

The Endangered Species Act (ESA)[1] provides for the listing and protection of species that are found to be "endangered" or "threatened"-species that need conservation efforts because they might become extinct. The listing of a species as endangered triggers the prohibitions in the Act against "taking (killing or harming) individuals of the protected species, unless a permit is obtained to take individuals incidental to an otherwise lawful proposed action, or unless an exemption for the proposed action is obtained. Unauthorized taking of a listed species can result in civil or criminal penalties. These prohibitions and potential penalties can affect various activities, including the use and development of land, with attendant economic impacts. Therefore, the extent to which likely economic impacts can be taken into account under the ESA has been of interest. Some parts of the Act relate to importation and commercial trading in listed species.[2] This report does not address those issues, but discusses the ESA generally and how

---

[1] Act of December 28, 1973, Pub. L. No. 93-205, 87 Stat. 884, codified at 16 U.S.C.§§ 1531 *et seq.*
[2] Note too that § 10(b) of the ESA and 50 C.F.R. §17.23 provide for "hardship exemptions" in some instances involving subsistence use or where a person had a contract to sell individuals of a listed species that predated the listing of that species and the person would suffer economic hardship if the contract were not carried out.

some of its provisions, aside from the commercial context, relate to the consideration of economic factors. It will be updated as circumstances warrant.

BACKGROUND

The ESA defines an "endangered species" as any species which is "in danger of extinction throughout all or a significant portion of its range." Excepted from this definition, however, are "species of the Class Insecta determined by the Secretary to constitute a pest whose protection under the provision of this chapter would present an overwhelming and overriding risk to man." This language appears to recognize the economic or health threats that some insects present. A "threatened species is one likely to become an endangered species within the foreseeable future throughout all or a significant portion of its range."

The Secretary of the Interior (with respect to terrestrial species) and the Secretary of Commerce (with respect to anadromous fish and certain other marine species) decide whether to list a species as endangered or threatened. The listing of a species triggers certain duties for federal agencies and applicants for federal permits, authorizations, or funding to consult with the Secretary (in practice either the Fish and Wildlife Service or the National Marine Fisheries Service respectively) if a proposed action may affect a listed species. This consultation will determine if the proposed action is likely to jeopardize the continued existence of a species or destroy or adversely modify habitat of a species determined by the Secretary to be critical.[3] If so, the Secretary is to suggest reasonable and prudent alternatives to the proposed action that would avoid jeopardizing the listed species.

Listing a species as endangered also means that the prohibitions of the ESA regarding the "taking" of endangered species apply. "Taking" means to harass, harm, pursue, hunt, shoot, wound, kill, trap, capture, or collect, or to attempt to engage in any such conduct.[4] The meaning of "harm" is elaborated on in regulations to include destruction of habitat severe enough to actually kill or injure wildlife by significantly impairing essential behavioral patterns, including breeding, feeding, or sheltering.[5] Current regulations provide that unless a special rule has been promulgated for a threatened species, threatened species shall receive the same protections as endangered species.[6] Exceptions to the taking

---

[3] 16 U.S.C. § 1536(a) and (b).
[4] 16 U.S.C. § 1532(19).
[5] 50 C.F.R. § 17.3.
[6] 50 C.F.R. § 17.31.

prohibitions are allowed as a result of either the consultation process under § 7 of the Act, or under the § 10 provisions that allow "incidental take permits" to be issued.

If a development or activity cannot be modified so that it avoids jeopardizing a listed species, the person or agency proposing the action must either desist, risk penalties for unlawful takes, or pursue the exemption process provided under the ESA to exempt that activity (not the species) from the penalties of the Act.

These aspects of the Act will be discussed in greater detail.

THE LISTING PROCESS

The determination of whether a species should be listed as endangered or threatened must be based on several factors that relate to the surviving numbers of a species and threats to its continued existence, but do not include a consideration of the economic effects of listing.[7] While the origins of threats to a species may be caused by development or other economic activities, listing determinations are expressly to be made "solely on the basis of the best scientific and commercial data available." The word "solely" was added in the 1982 amendments to the Act[8] to clarify that the determination of endangered or threatened status was intended to be made without reference to extraneous conditions such as economic factors. The committee reports elaborated on this point and also state that "commercial data" refers to trade data:

> ...The principal purpose of the amendments to Section 4 is to ensure that decisions pertaining to the listing and delisting of species are based solely upon biological criteria and to prevent non-biological considerations from affecting such decisions. To accomplish this and other purposes, Section 4(a) is amended in several instances...
> Section 4(b) of the Act is amended in several instances by Section 1(a)(2) of H.R. 6133. First, the legislation requires that the Secretary base his determinations regarding the listing or delisting of species "solely" on the basis of the best scientific and commercial data available to him. The addition of the word "solely" is intended to remove from the process of the listing or delisting of

---

[7] 16 U.S.C. § 1533(a)(1) states that a Secretary by regulation shall "determine whether any species is an endangered species or a threatened species because of any of the following factors:
(A)   the present or threatened destruction, modification, or curtailment of its habitat or range;
(B)   overutilization for commercial, recreational, scientific, or educational purposes;
(C)   disease or predation;
(D)   the inadequacy of existing regulatory mechanisms; or
(E)   other natural or manmade factors affecting its continued existence."
[8] Pub. L. No. 97-304, 96 Stat. 1411.

species any factor not related to the biological status of the species. The Committee strongly believes that economic considerations have no relevance to determinations regarding the status of species and intends that the economic analysis requirements of Executive Order 12291, and such statures as the Regulatory Flexibility Act and the Paperwork Reduction Act not apply. The Committee notes, and specifically rejects, the characterization of this language by the Department of the Interior as maintaining the status quo and continuing to allow the Secretary to apply Executive Order 12291 and other statutes in evaluating alternatives to listing. The only alternatives involved in the listing of species are whether the species should be listed as endangered or threatened or not listed at all. Applying economic criteria to the analysis of the alternatives and to any phase of the species listing process is applying economics to the determinations made under Section 4 of the Act and is specifically rejected by the inclusion of the word "solely" in this legislation.

Section 4(b) of the Act, as amended, provides that listing shall be based solely on the basis of the best "scientific and commercial data" available. The Committee did not change this information standard because of its interpretation of the word "commercial" to allow the use of trade data. Retention of the word "commercial" is not intended, in any way, to authorize the use of economic considerations in the process of listing a species.[9]

The conference report confirms that it was the intent of both chambers that economic factors not play a role in the listing of species for protection.

Section 2 of the Conference substitute amends section 4 of the Act in several ways. The principal purpose of these amendments is to ensure that decisions in every phase of the process pertaining to the listing or delisting of species are based solely upon biological criteria and to prevent non-biological considerations from affecting such decisions.[10]

The Committee of Conference (hereinafter the Committee) adopted the House language which requires the Secretary to base determinations regarding the listing or delisting of species "solely" on the bases of the best scientific and commercial data available to him. As noted in the House Report, economic considerations have no relevance to determinations regarding the status of species and the economic analysis requirements of Executive Order 12291, and such statutes as the Regulatory Flexibility Act and the Paperwork Reduction Act, will not apply to any phase of the listing process. The standards in the Act relating to the designation of critical habitat remain unchanged. The requirement that the Secretary consider for listing those species that states or foreign nations have designated or identified as in need of protection also remains unchanged.[11]

---

[9] H. R. Rep. No. 97-567 at 19-20 (1982).

[10] h. r. Rep. No. 97-835 at 19 (1982).

[11] *Ibid.,* at 20.

Therefore, the Act makes it clear that the decision as to whether a species is endangered or threatened is to be a scientific one in which economic factors do not play a part. Once this determination has been made, however, economic considerations may be, and in some instances must be, considered in analyzing what actions may be taken. This process has been analogized to making a diagnosis of whether a patient has cancer solely on medical grounds, but later considering economic factors in determining appropriate treatment once the patient has been diagnosed.

DESIGNATION OF CRITICAL HABITAT

In contrast to the process for listing a species as needing the protections of the ESA, in which process economic factors are not to play a part, economic factors expressly are to be considered in the designation of critical habitat for species. Concurrently with determining a species to be endangered or threatened, the Secretary "to the maximum prudent and determinable" is to designate the critical habitat of the species.[12]

When the Secretary designates critical habitat, the Secretary must do so:

On the basis of the best scientific data available and after taking into consideration the economic impact, and any other relevant impact, of specifying any particular area as critical habitat. The Secretary may exclude any area from critical habitat if he determines that the benefits of such exclusion outweigh the benefits of specifying such area as part of the critical habitat, unless he determines, base don the best scientific and commercial data available, that the failure to designate such area as critical habitat will result in the extinction of the species concerned.[13]

Therefore, although economic factors are not to be considered in the listing of a species as endangered or threatened, economic factors may enter into the designation of critical habitat, and some habitat areas may be excluded from

---

[12] 16 U.S.C. § 1533(a)(3). The reference to prudence reflects the fact that is necessary to take into account whether designating the habitat of a listed species would result in specimen collecting or other public intrusion into that habitat to the detriment of the species. The word "determinable" refers to whether it has been possible factually to determine the extent of the critical habitat. If the facts relevant to the designation of critical habitat are not yet available, the Secretary may postpone designation for an additional year. Eventually, habitat is to be designated to the maximum extent it is prudent to do so.

[13] 16 U.S.C. § 1533(b)(2).

designation based on such concerns, unless the failure to designate the habitat would result in the extinction of the subject species.

The significance of designating critical habitat is debatable. The Fish and Wildlife Service has asserted that designation does not add substantially to the protections afforded listed species, critical habitat designations are inordinately expensive compared to listing determinations, and that the agency would prefer not to use scarce resources to designate critical habitat. In fact, critical habitat has been designated for less than one fourth of listed species. On the other hand, modification of critical habitat may trigger § 7 consultation, may affect a finding of "harm," and may facilitate development of recovery plans.[14]

EXEMPTIONS

Federal agencies and non-federal persons may seek to have a particular action exempted from the penalties for taking endangered or threatened species in order to allow an activity or project to proceed even if that activity or project would destroy individuals of a listed species and might even jeopardize the continued existence of that species.

As originally enacted, the Act was an absolute prohibition against activities that would jeopardize endangered species. When the prospective impoundment of water behind the nearly completed Tellico dam threatened to eradicate the only known population of the snail darter (a small fish), the Supreme Court concluded that the "plan language" of the Act at that time mandated that the dam not operate.

> Concededly, this view of the Act will produce results requiring the sacrifice of thee anticipated benefit of the project and of many millions of dollars in public funds. But examination of the language, history, and structure of the legislation under review here indicates beyond doubt that Congress intended endangered species to be afforded the highest of priorities.[15]

After this Supreme Court decision, the ESA was amended to include a process by which economic impacts could be reviewed and projects exempted from the restrictions that otherwise would apply.[16] An "Endangered Species Committee" (Committee), consisting of specified Cabinet officials and one individual from each affected state reviews applications for exemptions. A federal

---

[14] See Pamela Baldwin, *The Role of Designation of Critical Habitat under the Endangered Species Act,* CRS Report for Congress RS20263, July 19, 1999.

[15] Tennessee Valley Authority v. Hill, 437 U.S. 153, 174 (1978).

[16] U.S.C. § 1536(e).

agency, the Governor of the state in which an agency action will occur, or a permit or license applicant may apply to the Secretary for an exemption. The application must describe the consultation process carried out and provide a statement as to why the proposed action cannot be modified to conform with the requirements of the statue.

To be eligible for an exemption the agency concerned and the exemption applicant must have carried out the consultation processes required under § 7 of the Act in good faith and must have made a reasonable and responsible effort to develop and fairly consider modifications or reasonable and prudent alternatives to the proposed action that do not jeopardize the continued existence of a listed species. They also must have conducted the required biological assessments and, to the extent determinable within the time provided, refrained from making any irreversible or irretrievable commitment of resources that would foreclose the formulation or implementation of reasonable and prudent alternative measures to avoid jeopardizing the species and habitat in question. These qualifying requirement are to ensure that the exemption process will not be preempted by the commitment of resources and preclusion of alternatives through actions already taken.

The Secretary, in consultation with the other members of the Committee, holds a hearing on the application and prepares a report. The report reviews whether the applicant has made any irreversible or irretrievable commitment of resources; discusses the availability of reasonable and prudent alternatives and the benefits of each. Provides a summary of the evidence concerning whether the action is in the public interest and is nationally or regionally significant; and outlines appropriate and reasonable mitigation and enhancement measures which should be considered by the Committee.[17]

The Committee then makes a final determination of whether to grant an exemption. The Committee shall grant an exemption if, based on the evidence, the Committee determines that:

(i)   there are no reasonable and prudent alternatives tot he agency action;
(ii) the benefits of such action clearly outweigh the benefits of alternative
(iii) courses of action consistent with conserving the species or its critical habitat, and such action is in the public interest;
(iv) the action is of regional or national significance; and
(v)   neither the federal agency concerned nor the exemption applicant made

---

[17] 16 U.S.C. § 1536 (g).

(vi) any irreversible or irretrievable commitment of resources prohibited by subsection (d) of this section [commitments as described above that jeopardize species or critical habitat].[18]

The Committee also must establish reasonable mitigation and enhancement measures as necessary and appropriate to minimize the adverse effects of an approved action on the species or critical habitat. These measures must be funded by the applicant.

An exemption must be granted for an agency action if the Secretary of Defense finds the exemption is necessary for reasons of national security.[19] The Committee may not grant an exemption that the Secretary of State finds would violate a treaty or other international obligation of the United States.[20] The President is authorized to make exemption determinations for a project for the repair or replacement of a public facility in a major disaster area if the President determines it is (1) necessary to prevent the recurrence of the natural disaster and to reduce the potential loss of human life, and (2) to involve an emergency situation which does not allow the ordinary procedures to be followed.[21]

An exemption is permanent unless the Secretary finds that the exemption would result in the extinction of a species that was not the subject of consultation, or was not identified in the biological assessment and the Committee determines that the exemption should not be permanent.[22]

The costs of required mitigation and enhancement measures specified in an approved exemption must be included in the overall costs of continuing the proposed action and the applicant must report annually to the Council on Environmental Quality on compliance with mitigation and enhancement measures.[23] The obligation to fund mitigation continues throughout the impacts of the exemption.

The Act expressly states that any action for which an exemption is granted is not to be considered a taking of any endangered species with respect to any activity necessary to carrying out the exempted action, and that any taking that is in compliance with the terms and conditions specified in a written statement issued by the Secretary after the consultation process is not to be considered a taking of the species concerned. In other words, the penalties that normally apply

---

[18] 16 U.S.C. § 1536(h).
[19] 16 U.S.C. § 1536(j).
[20] 16 U.S.C. § 1536(i).
[21] 16 U.S.C. § 1536(p).
[22] 16 U.S.C. § 1536(h).
[23] 16 U.S.C. § 1536(l).

to the taking of an endangered or threatened species do not apply to takings resulting from exempted actions.

There have been only a very few exemption applications filed and only two exemptions granted (one was in re the Grayrocks dam and the other was to approve 13 timber sales sought by the Bureau of Land Management in the Department of the Interior, but this latter exemption request was withdrawn before the completion of appeals). One application was denied (in re the Tellico dam, which was later allowed by Congress to proceed); one was dismissed as premature (in re the proposed Pittston oil refinery in Maine); and two others were withdrawn before Committee consideration.

One commentator has speculated that the low number of exemption applications may in part be because the process is rigorous, but also because the incentive to negotiate compromises is strong.

The main reasons for the low number of applications probably include the small number of jeopardy opinions issued, the stringent substantive standards for the grant of an exemption, and the complexity of the process. A likely additional factor is that most institutions, public or private, recognize that merely by seeking an exemption they risk being perceived as hostile to endangered species conservation. As long as public support for conservation is believed to be high, there is an incentive to compromise and avoid the need for an exemption.[24]

Another factor may be that the harm to a species resulting from an exempted action must be taken into account in reviewing other proposed actions that also may affect that species; more vigorous conservation actions may be necessary elsewhere to compensate for the exempted harm in order to recover the species in question. This fact also may make exemptions less desirable.

RECOVERY PLANS

Once a species is listed, the Secretary is to develop a recovery plan for that species that will assist the species in recovering to the point that the protection of the ESA is no longer needed. To the extent practicable, the Secretary is to develop recovery plans for those species that are most likely to benefit from such plans, "particularly those species that are, or may be, in conflict with construction or other development projects or other forms of economic activity;..." Recovery plans are to set goals for the conservation and survival of the species and set out

---

[24] Michael Beand and Melanie Rowland, THE EVOLUTION OF NATIONAL WILDLIFE LAW, 264-265 (3d Ed. 1998).

objective, measurable criteria that would result in a determination that the species could be removed from listing. A recovery plan also is to contain "estimates of the time required and the cost to carry out those measures needed to achieve the plan's goal and to achieve intermediate steps toward that goal."[25] Although all options must achieve recovery, the most cost-effective option may be selected.

ESA PROVISIONS WITH LESS DIRECT ECONOMIC EFFECTS

Other ESA provisions may involve economic factors less directly than those discussed above, especially as implemented administratively. Permit applicants may confer on possible impacts on species that have been proposed for listing and informal consultation is available with respect to preliminary project planning for actions that may affect a listed species. Both of these processes may assist with development of economic projects and activities so as to avoid both ESA conflicts and the expense of modifying actions later on. In addition, certain administrative actions afford landowners and developers greater certainty in moving forward with development activities.[26] These rules, combined with other agency policies and guidelines for improved processing of permit applications, have been seen by many as facilitating economic activities and development otherwise affected by the ESA.

---

[25] 16 U.S.C. § 1533(f).

[26] See the "No surprises" rule (63 Fed. Reg. 8859 (February 23, 1998)), which limits the changes the government can require a landowner to make to habitat conservation plans that are the basis for § 10 incidental take permits, and the "Safe harbor" agreements rule (64 Fed. Reg. 32706 (June 17, 1999)), which allows a landowner to make beneficial habitat improvements to land and later return to initial baseline conditions without penalties.

Chapter 2

THE CONVENTION ON INTERNATIONAL TRADE IN ENDANGERED SPECIES: ITS PAST AND FUTURE

M. Lynne Corn

INTRODUCTION[2]

In 1963, the General Assembly of the International Union for Conservation of Nature and Natural Resources (IUCN) called for an international convention on trade in animal species and their products. The request was a response to the impact that increased trade in animals, plants, and their products was having on wild populations of many species.

In March 1973, the Convention on International Trade in Endangered Species of Wild Fauna and Flora (CITES) met in Washington, D. C. At that time, 21 nations signed the treaty. CITES entered into force on July 1, 1975, 90 days after ten nations ratified the agreement. Currently, 122 nations are Parties to CITES. (See appendix A for a list of Party Nations and dates of entry.) The West African country of Mali may soon become the 123rd signatory.

CITES regulates international trade in animals and plants whose survival may be significantly threatened by trade. CITES operates on a permit system corresponding to species listed on three Appendices. Administrative bodies are the Secretariat, the Management and Scientific Authorities of each country, and

---

[2] Under the supervision of M. Lynn Corn. Cynthia Marcum, researched and contributed to this report.

the Conference of the Parties (COP). The Parties meet roughly every two years at a COP to evaluate implementation of the treaty and consider efforts which would improve CITES' success. In the United States, the Endangered Species Act (ESA; 16 U.S.C. 1531) is the implementing legislation for CITES. The Office of Management Authority (OMA) and the Office of Scientific Authority (OSA), in the Fish and Wildlife Service (FWS) in the Department of the Interior, exercise the responsibilities of the Management and Scientific Authorities. FWS (the Division of Law Enforcement), the Animal and Plant Health Inspection Service (APHIS) in the Department of Agriculture (for plant specimens), and the Customs Service in the Department of the Treasury have varying levels of enforcement responsibilities. The National Marine Fisheries Service in the Department of Commerce also has a small role in CITES" enforcement. While most agree the treaty has notably increased monitoring of animal and plant trade, it continues to face difficulties in implementation.

The next COP is scheduled for November 7-18, 1994, in Fort Lauderdale, Florida. A variety of issues are on the agenda, including adding several populations of saiga antelope to Appendix II, adding all North American box turtles (except the aquatic box turtle, which is already on Appendix I) to Appendix II, and discussing trade in whale and sharks products, listing criteria, and the status of rhinos and tigers. The listing of species of mahogany will also be addressed.

BACKGROUND

Basic Structure

Permit System
The permit system, as administered by the Management and Scientific Authorities, is the core of CITES. (See section below on Management and Scientific Authorities.) Any international trade of species on the Appendices requires proper permits or certificates of exemptions. Permits are given only if trade will not be detrimental to the survival of the species. Certificates of exemption are granted when trade in a species meets a set of criteria for exemption.

Both an import and an export permit (or re-export certificate; see Re-export Certificate below for definition) are required for the extremely limited trade allowed in Appendix I species. Trade in Appendix II species requires only an export permit, unless the importing country has imposed additional requirements, which is allowed under the treaty. International trade in Appendix III species may require one of three documents:

(1) *Export Permit:* granted for species coming from the country that listed it on Appendix III. For example, if Ghana chose to allow export of one of its Appendix III turtle doves (*Streptopelia turtur*), it would issue an export permit.

(2) *Re-export Certificate:* granted for Appendix III species being exported from a country that previously imported it. For example, if the United States allowed the import of a turtle dove from Ghana, which listed it originally, and then allowed its export, a re-export certificate would be issued.

(3) *Certificate of Origin:* issued by a country that did not list the species, but the specimen originated in that country. For example, if the United States wished to allow the export of a turtle dove hatched in the United States, a certificate of origin would be issued because this species was originally listed by Ghana. In this case, there is no requirement, to show that trade in the specimen would not be detrimental to the species' survival since it is not part of the original population that was listed.

A permit is not required for specimens being transported through a Party nation while the specimen remains in the control of customs officials, and under certain conditions, may be unnecessary for personal or household effects, not including live animals or plants. Moreover, if a Party enters, a "reservation," the transaction does not require a permit from or into the country taking the reservation, but would require a permit from the CITES signatory. A "reservation" occurs when a Party chooses to exempt itself from the Convention for certain species because it finds the listing of a particular species unacceptable. The Party is required to a bide by the rules of the Convention with regard to every other species except for those on which it has taken a reservation. Until a reservation is removed, that Party is treated as a non-Party state by other signatories for trade in that species.[2] As of October 1993, Liechtenstein and Switzerland had taken the greatest number of reservations, with 38 and 48 respectively. Notable reservations that are in effect are those by Japan and Norway for several species of whales.

---

[2] Article X of the treaty states: "Where export or re-export is to, or import is from, a State not a party to the present Convention, comparable documentation issued by the competent authorities in that State which substantially conforms with the requirements of the present Convention for permits and certificates may be acceptable in lieu thereof by any Party."

**Table 1. CITES Documents which Must be Presented to the FWS
(for animals) or APHIS Inspector (for plants) at the U.S. Port for Import,
Export, or Re-export of CITES Species**

	Appendix I	Appendix II	Appendix III
IMPORT to United States	1) original foreign export permit or re-export certificate 2) original U.S. import permit	1) original foreign export permit or re-export certificate	1) original foreign export permit, re-export certificate, or Certificate of Origin
EXPORT /RE-EXPORT out of the United States	1) original U.S. export permit or re-export certificate 2) copy of foreign (if specimen is being re-exported)	1) original U.S. export permit or re-export certificate	1) original U.S. Certificate of Origin or re-export certificate

Source: U.S. Department of the Interior, Fish and Wildlife Service. Fish & Wildlife Facts. 1993

Exemptions

In certain situations, Certificates of Exemption may be issued, rather than permits. Certificates of Exemption are issued for pre-convention specimens or the species that are part of scientific exchanges. Pre-convention specimens are those specimens acquired before the Convention's application to the species. Scientific exchange is the non-commercial exchange of specimens between registered scientific institutions. Management Authorities may waive the permit or certificate requirement for specimens that are part of a traveling zoo, circus, plant exhibition, or other traveling exhibition.

Appendices

Under CITES, species are listed in Appendices I, II, or III. Any species, subspecies, or geographically separate population can be listed. Article II of the treaty provides conditions under which species are to be included in each appendix. It states:

Appendix I shall include all species threatened with extinction which are or may be affected by trade. Trade in specimens of these species must be subject to particularly strict regulation in order not to endanger further their survival and must only be authorized in exceptional circumstances.

Circumstances under which these species may be traded include: scientific exchange, breeding, or for educational programs. For example, trade in the

California condor (*Gymnogyps californianus*) might be permitted for captive breeding purposes, provided that the survival of the species would not be threatened by the trade.

Article II defines Appendix II species to include:

(a) all species which although not necessarily now threatened with extinction may become so unless trade in specimens of such species is subject to strict regulation in order to avoid utilization incompatible with their survival; and

(b) other species which must be subject to regulation in order that trade in specimens of certain species referred to in sub-paragraph (a) of this paragraph may be brought under effective control.

Trade in Appendix II species is less restrictive than trade in species listed under Appendix I, and exchange is permitted for commercial purposes. For example, until 1989, when the African elephant was moved from Appendix II to Appendix I, African elephant products were traded freely on the international market.

To list a species under Appendices I or II, information is required on populations size, geographic range, habitat destruction, trade, or other possible conditions that could severely reduce its population or lead to extinction. In certain cases, CITES treats individuals or parts of Appendix I species as Appendix II species if they have been bred in captivity or artificially propagated.

Article II also states:

Appendix III shall include all species which any Party identifies as being subject to regulation within its jurisdiction for the purpose of preventing or restricting exploitation, and as needing the cooperation of other parties in the control of trade.

It is important to note that while inclusion in Appendices I and II requires a vote of the Parties, inclusion in Appendix III does not. (See section below on Conference of the Parties.)

While listing a species may appear demanding, "down-listing" (either removing a species from the Appendices or moving it from Appendix I to Appendix II) is also difficult. A resolution adopted at the first CITES Conference of the Parties in 1976 provides that a species may be down-listed under one of two conditions:

(1) either the population has recovered sufficiently so that either protection under CITES is no longer necessary or less stringent trade restrictions would suffice, or

(2) the original data were incorrect and the species should never have been listed.

CITES has generally been cautious about down-listing species and it requires convincing scientific evidence before doing so. This evidence may include studies on population and analyses of the possibility for commercial trade and of its imports.

Administration

The administration of CITES is divided into the Secretariat, the Management and Scientific Authorities, and the Conference of the Parties. Originally the Untied Nations Environment Programme (UNEP) took financial responsibility for administration of the treaty, but as CITES grew, the need for self-sufficiency became apparent. Eventually a Trust Fund was established ,and CITES signatories may contribute to it. The Fund is still managed by UNEP.

Secretariat

The Secretariat, now located in Geneva, Switzerland encompasses the administrative staff of CITES as a whole, and is headed by a Secretary-General. Though the Secretary-General is hired through UNEP, he/she cannot be hired or fired without agreement of the Parties.

The Secretariat has a broad range of duties. It organizes meetings of the Parties, prepares reports for those meetings, publishes annual reports on the work and accomplishments of the convention, and contracts for scientific and technical studies to aid CITES' implementation. The Secretariat is also responsible for directing the attention of the Parties to issues that may affect implementation, printing up-to-date editions of the Appendices, studying Party reports, making recommendations to members, and performing other duties that may be assigned to it by the Parties.

Management and Scientific Authorities

The Management Authorities have been assigned the responsibility for granting or denying CITES permits. Parties have developed their Management Authorities along different lines. For example, some countries have divided responsibilities on the basis of the type of documentation needed, and other countries on whether the specimen being traded is plant or animal. Qualifications for granting or denying a permit vary according to the Appendix. In general, the management Authority must determine that:

(1) the specimen was not obtained through the violation of any domestic laws,

(2) a living specimen will be prepared and shipped in a manner not detrimental to its health or welfare,

(3) an import permit has been granted for Appendix I species before an export permit can be granted, and

(4) import of specimens on Appendix I is not primarily for commercial purposes.

(5) The necessary advice from the Scientific Authority has been issued.

Management Authorities are also responsible for confiscated live specimens (plants and animals). The specimens are to be sent to the State of origin, a rescue center, or some other suitable site, such as a zoo. Furthermore, to help prevent forgery of documents, Management Authorities must supply copies of stamps, seals, etc. used on its permits to any Party that requests a copy.

The Scientific Authorities advise the Management Authorities about whether trade will endanger a species' survival. Management Authorities may not issue an import or export permit without first obtaining this information. In addition, the Scientific Authorities advise whether the person or entity receiving the specimen will be able to care for it properly. The Scientific Authorities also recommend to the management Authorities measures to limit issuance of permits to avoid listing specimens on Appendix I. Advice is to be based on information on the population status, distribution, harvest, population trends, other ecological or biological information, and the possibility for trade. The Scientific Authorities are further directed to review the qualifications of scientific organizations pursuing registration for scientific exchanges.

Conferences of the Parties

CITES requires that a COP convene once every two years, unless more or less frequent Conferences are agreed upon by the Parties. At these Conferences, the Parties are to evaluate the implementation of CITES and make necessary financial provisions to enable the Secretariat to perform its duties. The Parties also deliberate and adopt amendments to the Appendices, review the recovery and conservation of listed species, review and consider reports presented by the

Secretariat or any Party, and make recommendations for improving CITES implementation.

Attendance of the Conference of the Parties is not limited to Party members. There is an open invitation for the Untied Nations, its specialized agencies, the International Atomic Energy Agency, and non-member States to attend. Also, any international or national body (governmental or not), that is "technically qualified in protection, conservation or management of wild fauna and flora" may send observers.[3] The latter must obtain approval from their Management Authority and notify the Secretariat of intent to attend a Conference and may be excluded from attendance if one-third of the Parties protest a certain organization's presence. While all present may participate, only Party nations can vote.

There have been eight COPs since the Convention convened in 1973. The next is scheduled in the United States from November 7-18, 1994. (See Table 2.)

Table 2. Conferences of the Parties

COP	Site	Date
COP1	Berne, Switzerland	November 1976
COP2	San Jose, Costa Rica	March 1979
COP3	New Delhi, India	February 1981
COP4	Gaborone, Botswana	April 1983
COP5	Buenos Aires, Argentina	April 1985
COP6	Ottawa, Canada	July 1987
COP7	Lausanne, Switzerland	October 1989
COP8	Kyoto, Japan	March 1992
COP9	Fort Lauderdale, Florida	November 1994

Kyoto, Japan, Conference

The eighth COP was in Kyoto, Japan, in March 1992. It was attended by 101 Party nations, 5 non-party nations, UNEP, the European Economic Community, and 155 other international and national organizations. At the Conference, 23 resolutions were adopted, and the foremost topics were the wild bird trade, bluefin tuna (*Thunnus thynnus*), and the African elephant (*Loxodonta africana*). Conflicting views over criteria to decide on proposed listings, up-listings, or de-listings were also expressed.

---

[3] Article XI, section 7.

Under CITES, living specimens are required to be shipped so as to minimize harm or injury to health, but there has been a continuing high mortality of some species, particularly birds, since the inception of CITES. The Parties agreed to seek information to minimize mortality and to submit records of mortalities for shipments of birds.

Sweden had proposed listing the bluefin tuna in the Eastern Atlantic on Appendix II and those in the Western Atlantic on Appendix I. The United States opposed this proposal on the grounds that decrease in tuna fishing quotas and improvements in documentation of trade by the International Commission for the Conservation of Atlantic Tunas would sufficiently promote the bluefin's recovery. Sweden eventually withdrew its proposal.

One proposal was submitted by Botswana, Malawi, Namibia, South Africa, and Zimbabwe. These five nations proposed to sown-list their African Elephant populations from Appendix I to Appendix II. At COP7, all African elephants had been placed on Appendix I due to poaching for ivory. In Kyoto, the Parties agreed to leave all populations on Appendix I. As a result of the rejection, these African nations chose to take a reservation. The five nations will be permitted to trade African elephant products only with either non-party nations or with other nations that have taken a reservation on the African elephant, of which there are none outside of Africa. As of August 1993, the reservations were still in place. The practical benefit of these reservations to the five nations is speculative since the major markets for ivory products are outside their boundaries.

Committees

Over the years, the Parties agreed that achieving CITES' goals required more than biennial meetings. Several Committees were created that meet more frequently. Five permanent committees exist: the Standing Committee, the Plant Committee, the Animal Committee, the Nomenclature Committee, and the Identification Committee.

The Standing Committee focuses on budget, administrative, and internal affairs, and is composed of six representatives (as elected by their respective regions), a representative from the depository government (Switzerland), and delegates from the host countries of the previous and upcoming COPs. The Plant and Animal Committees, each having six regional representatives, advise the COPs on plant and animal issues respectively, review Appendix II species trade data, and reassess the condition of listed species to determine if continued protection is warranted. Membership in the Nomenclature and Identification Committees is voluntary, and for each, a Chairperson and Vice-Chairperson are elected. The Nomenclature Committee concentrates on developing and maintaining standardized nomenclature for all listed species. The Identification Committee gathers information to assist in identification of specimens and parts for customs officials.

Enforcement

Under Article VIII, Party nations agree to engage in a number of enforcement activities. Each Party is to establish legislation implementing CITES, including penalizing trade activities that violate the provisions of the treaty. Parties are also required to confiscate specimens (living or dead) which are being illegally traded. If the specimens are living, Management Authorities are responsible for their care, by sending them either to the State of origin or to some other suitable site for their care. Dead specimens may be sent to museums or to facilities that train enforcement officers in identification. Seized Appendix I specimens may not be put into commercial trade.

Under CITES each Party is to compile and submit a detailed annual record of exports and imports of listed species. Parties are further required to produce biennial reports on the regulatory, administrative, and legislative actions they have taken to enforce CITES.

The treaty also suggests Party nations specify special ports of exit and entry for all animal and plant specimens that pass through the nation. While few nations have actually implemented this recommendation, evidence from Party nations that have suggests it has been beneficial in curbing illegal trade. The United States has designated 13 ports: Baltimore, Los Angeles, New York/Newark, Chicago, Miami, Portland (OR), Dallas/Ft. Worth, New Orleans, San Francisco, Honolulu, New York/JFK, Seattle, and Boston. Additional ports for plants have also been designated, some specifically for ginseng, orchids, and timbers.

In the United States, the FWS Division of Law Enforcement, the Customs Service, and APHIS (for plants only) are responsible for enforcement.

CITES AND THE ESA

The Endangered Species Act (ESA) implements CITES in the United States. While there are similarities between CITES and the ESA, there are important differences. They are similar in that listed species are divided into groups based on relative threat of extinction to the species. CITES has three Appendices, while the ESA has two lists: endangered and threatened. However, CITES and the ESA differ in protective measures. CITES focuses only on regulating international trade, while the ESA considers additional threats, such as habitat loss. The standards for listing under CITES and the ESA also differ substantially. (See Article II of the treaty and section 4(a) of the ESA. The difference between a "threatened" listing and Appendix II status is particularly notable.)

Although there is no legal requirement connecting listing under CITES and the ESA, the lists overlap considerably among certain animal taxa. Even species listed under CITES but not under the ESA, such as the Northern Goshawk (*Accipiter gentiles)* are protected in the United States to the extent that they are traded across U.S. borders. Many foreign species are listed under CITES Appendix I, but due to other pressing matters have not yet been subject to an ESA status review for possible listing under U.S. law.

IMPLEMENTATION: SUCCESSES AND PROBLEMS

Successes

CITES is one of the world's most widely accepted international treaties with 122 signatories. (See Appendix A for a list of signatories.) Many believe it has notably increased monitoring and control of animal and plant trade (estimated at over $5 billion a year) and awareness of the impact of international trade on wild populations.[4] Furthermore, many Parties recognize that continued trade in species depends on preventing over-exploitation. While it seems certain that many species would be in a worse state without CITES' protection, it is extremely difficult to point to the treaty and identify it as the sole reason for a species' continued existence. Some species may benefit from the attention and funding through inclusion in CITES. One success story is the stabilization of African elephant populations. The population began to level at approximately 600, 000 in 1989, after falling from 1.2 million in 1979. The 1989 decision by Party nations to ban all trade in African elephant ivory and hides has been credited with helping populations recover.

---

[4] Balistrieri, Carlo. "CITES: The ESA and International Trade," *Natural Resources & Environment,* Summer 1993: 33-35, 74-76

Problems

Difficulties with Implementation
   While implementations of CITES has been successful in some respects, numerous obstacles and problems with the treaty have been noted. First, while Parties are obligated to establish Management and Scientific Authorities, many of the developing countries have had difficulty in staffing, training, and equipping these Authorities. Some Parties have yet to designate a Scientific Authority, and the Scientific Authorities in many countries lack independence. Even under good administration, obtaining the necessary biological information (some of the information needed to justify granting or denying a permit), such as population levels, can be impractical or even impossible.

   Another serious problem is the ease with which shipments of legal and illegal specimens can be confused. Even the most highly qualified enforcement officers may have trouble distinguishing among similar specimens, especially in the form of handbags, wallets, shoes, etc. It is particularly easy to confuse legal and illegal shipments of reptile products. An estimated 30 percent of the total value of international animal trade is composed of illegally traded species.[5]

   Many believe the mild penalties for violations are also an implementation obstacle. CITES does not provide any guidance on the level of penalties to impose, so there is substantial variation in how Parties penalize. In many countries the penalties are either nonexistent or so low that they may not even affect the illegal trader. However, confiscation, which is required under the treaty, can be a significant penalty.

   Some feel that simply listing species on the Appendices may be counterproductive. Listing can be an advertisement for rarity and may actually increase trade. When two orchid general, Asian tropical lady's slippers (*Paphiopedilum spp.*), were listed, interest and demand for the species actually increased. A similar phenomenon has been noted under the ESA, where the listing of certain cactus species, for example, has increased demand for those species.

   Another dilemma concerns reports that are to be submitted by Parties. These reports are often late, incomplete, in the wrong format, or not submitted at all. Reasons for these problems range from difficulty in getting the data from customs to a lack of technical, financial, legislative, or administrative support, especially in developing countries. As a result, it is difficult for nations to establish the effect of trade on the status of a species.

---

[5] Misch, Ann. "Can Wildlife Traffic Be Stopped?" *World Watch*, Sept.-Oct. 1992: p. 26, 33.

Many critics believe a major threat to effective implementation of CIYES is the ability of a Party to take a "reservation." Taking a reservation permits a Party to exempt itself from the CITES requirements in regard to species the Party objects to having listed on the Appendices. Once a party has taken a reservation, it is treated as a non-party nation for the purpose of trade in that species. Therefore, a Party that takes a reservation on a species may trade that species with non-party nations or with other Parties taking a reservation on the same species. Through reservations must be taken when the Party accedes to the Convention or immediately after amendments to the Appendices have been adopted, they may be withdrawn at any time. It is possible for trade in certain species to continue practically unregulated, and become threatening to the species' survival. For example, if the Republic of Korea, which has taken a reservation on all bears listed under Appendix II, continues to trade in bear parts with non-parties, such as Taiwan, bear populations around the world could be threatened, especially if such trade is used as a cover for illegal trade. Supporters of the reservation provisions in CITES counter that a country's only alternative to a reservation would otherwise be dropping out of CITES entirely, and thereby possibly failing to protect or monitor any listed species.

Finally, and most broadly, many observers note the general lack of will in some nations to enforce CITES. There many be inadequate scrutiny of permits, acceptance of bribes, failure to fund adequate staffing, and a host of other problems. CITES has devoted relatively little attention to this problem and the past COPs have considered the issue only sporadically. It generally arises only when it reaches high levels in a particular species. (See discussion of People's Republic of China and Taiwan certifications, below.)

Issues Not Covered by the Treaty

Complicating the issue of CITES' success is the lack of provisions in CITES to apply mandatory sanctions against a member who is failing to comply with the treaty. However, the Conference of the Parties and the Standing Committee have recommended sanctions on a number of occasions. These have usually been implemented by a small number of Parties.

The United States, for example, currently enforces a ban on Thai animal product imports. In the past, the United States has certified nations under authority of the Pelly Amendments to the Fishermen's Protective Act of 1967, as amended (22 U.S.C. 1978 (a)(4). Certification results when the Secretary of the Interior or the Secretary of Commerce finds that nationals of a foreign nation are engaging in activities that diminish the effectiveness of an international program designed to protect endangered species. Certification can lead to a U.S. embargo on trade in certain animal products from that country. In the past, certification has always been enough to bring dissenting countries into line with international conservation efforts; an actual embargo has never been necessary.[6]

Certification was used most recently when the Secretary of the Interior certified the People's Republic of China (PRC) and Taiwan in September 1993 for their continuing trade in rhino and tiger products. While the PRC is a signatory of CITES, Taiwan is not. In April 1994, the President announced his decision to impose trade sanctions against Taiwan, but not the PRC. Some observers felt his decision to forego trade sanctions against the PRC was based more on a hope of maintaining cooperation both on human rights and on U.S. efforts to persuade North Korea to open its nuclear facilities to international inspection than on Chinese animal protection efforts. On August 9, 1994, the inspection than on Chinese animal protection efforts. August 9, 1994, the Presidential memorandum announcing the implementation of the ban against Taiwan was published in the Federal Register (59 CFR 40463). Import restrictions are imposed on such products as reptile leather shoes, handbags, and other reptile leather product; live goldfish and tropical fish for the aquarium trade; bird feathers, down, and specimens; and jewelry made from coral, bone, and mussel shells. The ban, which was to have entered into force on August 19, 1994, will remain in effect until Taiwan makes "sufficient progress" in curbing illegal trade in tiger and rhino parts.

In 1980, Japan signed CITES and at that time took reservations on several species of sea turtles. Japan continued rather high volumes of trade in sea turtle products and eventually was found to have been trading with countries that have export bans on sea turtle products. This meant that Japan was interfering with international and domestic efforts to save the sea turtles. As a result, Japan was certified by the Secretary of the interior and the Secretary of Commerce in March 1991. Japan announced in June 1991 that it would begin to reduce imports of the hawksbill sea turtle (*Eretmochelys imbricata),* one of the species on which Japan had taken a reservation, and by December 31, 1992, it apparently stopped all sea turtle imports. As a result, trade sanctions were never imposed.

Another commonly cited problem is the lack of internal regulation in the treaty. CITES is only concerned with international trade and its effect on species. It makes no requirement for countries to address internal problems, such as habitat loss, which may often be a greater threat to a species than international trade.

---

[6] The use of certification and other international trade restrictions is controversial, and has been attacked by some as a violation of the General Agreement of Tariffs and Trade (GATT). For a discussion of this issue, see CRS Rept. 91-666, *Tuna and the GATT.*

Moreover, CITES fails to address domestic trade, which may also be very threatening to a species' survival.

UPCOMING EVENTS

The ninth Conference of the Parties meeting is scheduled to take place November 7-18, 1994, in Fort Lauderdale, Florida. The United States has submitted its proposed resolutions and amendments to the Appendices. Proposed resolutions include new criteria for amending the Appendices and standardizing nomenclature. Proposed amendments to the Appendices include changing the Mongolian population of saiga antelope (*Saiga tatarica*) from Appendix II to Appendix I; adding all other populations of saiga antelope to Appendix II; including all species of tarantulas *(Brachyelma spp.)* in Appendix II and including all North American box turtles (*Terrapene spp.*) on Appendix II, except for the aquatic box turtle *(T. coahuila),* which is already on Appendix I. The transfer of Urial sheep (*Ovis vignei*), except *Ovis vignei vignei*, from Appendix I to Appendix II will also be considered. The United States has also proposed discussing trade in whale and shark products.

As of July 20, 1994, 40 U.S. organizations have been granted approval to attend COP9. Included in this list is the African Wildlife Foundation, Defenders of Wildlife, Earthrust, the Humane Society of the United States, the National Rifle Association of America, and World Wildlife Fund.

While the Secretariat has not yet received all proposals by the Parties, many have been submitted a resolution to establish a formal law enforcement consultation network to operate between COPs. The United Kingdom also offered a resolution to improve future law enforcement communications. Proposals from other Parties to amend the Appendices include three proposals to list "mahoganies" in Appendix II (submitted by Germany and the Netherlands). South Africa has proposed down-listing its population of African elephants (*Loxodonta africana)* from Appendix I to Appendix II, and the Sudan offered a similar proposal for its African elephant population.

APPENDIX A: LIST OF PARTY COUNTRIES
TO CITES (AS OF 5/15/94)[7]

Parties (Date of Entry)

Afghanistan (1/28/86)	Germany (6/20/76)	Peru (9/25/75)
Algeria (2/21/84)	Ghana (2/12/76)	Philippines (11/16/81)
Argentina (4/8/81)	Greece (1/6/93)	Poland (3/12/90)
Australia (10/27/76)	Guatemala (2/5/80)	Portugal (3/11/81)
Bahamas (9/18/79)	Guinea (12/20/81)	Russian Federation (12/8/76)
Bangladesh (2/18/82)	Guinea-Bissau (8/14/90)	Rwandese Republic (1/18/81)
Barbados (3/9/93)	Guyana (8/25/77)	Saint Kitts and Nevis (5/15/94)
Belgium (1/1/984)	Honduras (6/13/85)	Saint Lucia (3/15/83)
Belize (9/21/81)	Hungary (8/27/85)	Saint Vincent and the Grenadines (2/28/89)
Benin (5/28/84)	India (10/18/76)	
Bolivia (10/4/79)	Indonesia (3/28/79)	Senegal (11/3/77)
Botswana (2/12/78)	Iran (11/1/76)	Seychelles (5/9/77)
Brazil (11/14/75)	Israel (3/17/80)	Singapore (2/28/87)
Brunei Darussalem (8/2/90)	Italy (12/31/79)	Slovakia (1/1/93)
Bulgaria (4/16/91)	Japan (11/4/80)	Somalia (3/2/86)
Burkina Faso (1/11/90)	Jordon (3/14/79)	South Africa (10/13/75)
Burundi (11/6/88)	Kenya (3/13/79)	Spain (8/28/86)
Cameroon (9/31/81)	Korea, Republic of (10/7/93)	Sri Lanka (8/2/79)
Canada (7/9/75)	Liberia (6/9/81)	Sudan (1/24/83)
Central African Republic (11/25/80)	Liechtenstein (2/28/80)	Suriname (2/15/81)
Chad (5/3/89)	Luxembourg (3/12/84)	Sweden (7/1/75)
Chile (7/1/75)	Madagascar (11/18/75)	Switzerland (7/1/75)
China, People's Republic Of (4/8/81)	Malawi (5/6/82)	Tanzania (2/27/80)
Colombia (11/29/81)	Malaysia (1/18/78)	Thailand (4/21/83)
Congo (5/1/83)	Malta (7/16/89)	Togo (1/21/79)
Costa Rica (9/28/75)	Mauritius (7/27/75)	Trinidad and Tobago (4/19/84)
Cuba (7/19/90)	Mexico (9/30/91)	Tunisia (7/1/75)
Cyprus (7/1/75)	Monaco (7/18/78)	Uganda (10/16/91)

[7] List obtained from the Office of Management Authority, U.S. Fish and Wildlife Service, Department of the Interior. There were 122 signatories as of August 10, 1994. Mali, in West Africa, is expected to become a Party shortly.

Czech Republic (1/1/93)	Morocco (1/14/76)	United Arab Emirates (5/9/90)
Denmark (10/24/77)	Mozambique (6/23/81)	United Kingdom (10/31/76)
Djibouti (5/7/92)	Namibia (3/18/91)	U.S.A.(7/1/75)
Dominican Republic (3/17/87)	Nepal (9/16/75)	Uruguay (7/1/75)
Ecuador (7/1/75)	Netherlands (7/18/75)	Vanuatu (10/15/89)
Egypt (4/4/78)	New Zealand (8/8/89)	Venezuela (1/22/78)
El Salvador (7/29/87)	Nicaragua (11/4/77)	Viet Nam(4/20/94)
Equatorial Guinea (6/8/92)	Niger (12/7/75)	Zaire (10/18/76)
Estonia (10/20/92)	Nigeria (7/1/75)	Zambia (2/22/81)
Ethiopia (7/4/89)	Norway (10/25/76)	Zimbabwe (8/17/81)
Finland (8/8/76)	Pakistan (7/19/76)	
France (8/9/78)	Panama (11/15/78)	
Gabon (5/15/89)	Papua New Guinea (3/11/76)	
Gambia (11/24/77)	Paraguay (2/13/77)	

APPENDIX B: ACRONYMS

APHIS	U.S. Animal and Plant Health Inspection Service
CITES	Convention on International Trade in Endangered Species of Wild Fauna and Flora
COP	Conference of the Parties
ESA	U.S. Endangered Species Act
FWS	U.S. Fish and Wildlife Service
IUCN	International Union for Conservation of Nature and Natural Resources
NMFS	U.S. National Marine Fisheries Service
OMA	Office of Management Authority
OSA	Office of Scientific Authority
PRC	People's Republic of China
UNEP	United Nations Environment Programme

Chapter 3

ENDANGERED SPECIES ACT:
THE LISTING AND EXEMPTION PROCESSES

M. Lynne Corn and Pamela Baldwin

INTRODUCTION

The Endangered Species ACT (the ESA)[1] provides for the listing and protection of species that are currently endangered or threatened with extinction. The listing of a species results in limitations on activities that could affect that species and in penalties for the "taking" of individuals of a listed species. The listing process is based on scientific considerations only, but economic factors may enter into *other* decisions under the ESA. The principal vehicle by which economic factors may be considered is the exemption process whereby a specially convened committee may exempt certain actions from the prohibitions of the ESA. This report discusses the Endangered Species Act and how the listing and exemption procedures work. Figure 1 of this report depicts in graphic form how an application proceeds through the exemption process.

Because of the current controversy surrounding the proposed listing of the northern spotted own in the Pacific Northwest and possible economic impacts to that region, the report will focus on that species.

---

[1] Act of December 28, 1973, Pub. L. No. 93-205, 87 Stat. 884, codified at 16 U.S.C. 1531 *et seq.*

Listing of Species

The ESA defines an "endangered species" as any species which is "in danger of extinction throughout all or a significant portion of its range." A "threatened" species is one that is likely to become endangered.

The Secretary of the Interior, and in certain instances, the Secretary of Commerce decide whether to list a species as endangered or threatened. ("The Secretary" in this report means the appropriate Secretary, that in the spotted owl context is the Secretary of the Interior.) Because the ESA defines species as meaning either a species, a subspecies, or, for vertebrates only, a population,[2] there is some flexibility as to how to provide different levels of protection to less than a whole species. The listing of a species triggers certain duties for Federal agencies and applicants for Federal permits, authorizations, or funding to consult with the Secretary of the Interior (in actual practice, the Fish and Wildlife Service) as to reasonable and prudent alternatives to actions that would jeopardize a species or adversely modify its habitat.[3] Listing also results in prohibitions or limitations on certain actions that may be taken if doing so would adversely affect a listed species. Furthermore, the ESA contains penalties for the "taking" of a listed species. "Taking" is defined very broadly as including harassing, harming, pursuing, hunting, shooting, wounding, killing, trapping, capturing, or collecting, or attempting to engage in any such conduct.[4]

The determination of whether a species should be listed as endangered or threatened must be based on several scientific factors related to a species and threats to its continuance. The ESA expressly states that listing determinations are to be made "solely on the basis of the best scientific and commercial data available."[5] The word "solely" was added in the 1982 amendments to the ESA[6] to

---

[2] 16 U.S.C. 1532 (16).
[3] 16 U.S.C. 1536(a) and (b).
[4] 16 U.S.C. 1532(19).
[5] 16 U.S.C. 1533(a)(1) states that the Secretary by regulation shall "determine whether any species is an endangered species or a threatened species because of any of the following factors:
　　(A) the present or threatened destruction, modification, or curtailment of hits habitat or range;
　　(B) overutilization for commercial, recreational, scientific, or educational purposes;
　　(C) disease or predation;
　　(D) the inadequacy of existing regulatory mechanisms; or
　　(E) other natural or manmade factors affecting its continued existence."
16 U.S.C. 1533(b)(1)(A) states in full: "The Secretary shall make determinations required by subsection (a)(1) of this section solely on the bases of the best scientific and commercial data available to him after conducting a review of the status of the species and after taking into account those efforts, if any, being made by any State or foreign nation, to protect such species, whether by

clarify that the determination of endangered or threatened status was intended to be made without reference to economic factors:

> ...The principal purpose of the amendments to Section 4 is to ensure that decisions pertaining to the listing and delisting of species are based solely upon biological criteria and to prevent non-biological considerations from affecting such decisions. To accomplish this and other purposes, Section 4(a) is amended in several instances.
>
> Section 4(b) of the Act is amended in several instances by Section 1(a)(2) of H.R. 6133. First, the legislation requires that the Secretary base his determinations regarding the listing or delisting of species "solely" on the basis of the best scientific and commercial data available to him. The addition of the word "solely" is intended to remove from the process of this listing or delisting of species any factor not related to the biological status of the species. The Committee strongly believes that economic considerations have no relevance to determinations regarding to the status of species and intends that the economic analysis requirements of Executive Order 12291, and such statutes as the Regulatory Flexibility Act and the Paperwork Reduction Act not apply. The Committee notes, and specifically rejects, the characterization of this language by the Department of the Interior as maintaining the status quo and continuing to allow the Secretary to apply Executive Order 12291 and other statutes in evaluating alternatives to listing. The only alternatives involved in the listing of species are whether the species should be listed as endangered or threatened or not listed at all. Applying economic criteria to the analysis for these alternatives and to any phase of the species listing process is applying economics to the determinations made under Section 4 of the Act and is specifically rejected by the inclusion of the word "solely" in this legislation.
>
> Section 4(b) of the Act, as amended, provides that listings shall be based solely on the basis of the best "scientific and commercial data" available. The Committee did not change this information standard because of its interpretation of the word "commercial" to allow the use of trade data. Retention of the word "commercial" is not intended, in any way, to authorize the use of economic considerations in the process of listing a species.[7]

The Conference report confirms that it was the intent of both chambers that economic factors not play a role in the designation and listing of species for protection.

> Section 2 of the Conference substitute amends section 4 of the Act in several ways. The principal purpose of these amendments is to ensure that decisions in every phase of the process pertaining to the listing or delisting of species are

---

predator control, protection of habitat and food supply, or other conservation practices, within any area under its jurisdiction, or on the high seas."

[6] Act of October 13, 1982, Pub. L. 97-304, 96 Stat. 1411.

[7] H.R. Rep. No. 567, 97th Cong., 2d Sess. 19-20 (1982).

based solely upon biological criteria and to prevent non-biological considerations from affecting such decisions.[8]

The Committee of Conference (hereinafter the Committee) adopted the House language which requires the Secretary to base determinations regarding the listing or delisting of species "solely" on the basis of the best scientific and commercial data available to him. As noted in the House Report, economic considerations have no relevance to determinations regarding the status of species and the economic analysis requirements of Executive Order 12291, and such statutes as the Regulatory Flexibility Act and the Paperwork Reduction Act, will not apply to any phase of the listing process. The standards in the Act relating to the designation of critical habitat remain unchanged. The requirement that the Secretary consider for listing those species that states or foreign nations have designated or identified as in need of protection also remains unchanged.

The Committee adopted, with modifications, the Senate amendments which combined and rewrote section 4(b) and (f) of the Act to streamline the listing process by reducing the time periods for rulemaking, consolidating public meeting and hearing requirements and establishing virtually identical procedures for the listing and delisting of species and for the designation of critical habitat.[9]

In summary, the ESA makes clear that whether a species is endangered or threatened is a scientific question in which economic factors do not play a part. Once this determination is made, however, economics then may be considered in analyzing some possible subsequent actions.

Designation of Critical Habitat

In contrast to the listing process in which economic factors are not to play a part, economic factors expressly may enter in to the designation of critical habitat for species. Concurrently with determining a species to be endangered or threatened, the Secretary "to the maximum extent prudent and determinable"[10] is to designate the critical habitat of the species. The reference to the designation of critical habitat being "prudent" reflects the need to take into account whether designating habitat would harm the species, for example by specimen collecting, etc. If the facts relevant to the designation of critical habitat are not yet "determinable," the Secretary may postpone habitat designation for an additional year. Eventually, habitat is to be designated to the maximum extent it is prudent to do so.[11]

---

[8] H.R. Rep. No. 835, 97th Cong., 2d Sess. 19 (1982).
[9] Id., at 20.
[10] 16 U.S.C. 1533(a)(3).
[11] 16 U.S.C. 1533(b)(6)(C).

If the Secretary designates critical habitat, the Secretary must do so

On the basis of the best scientific data available and after taking into consideration the economic impact, and any other relevant impact, of specifying any particular area as critical habitat. The Secretary may exclude any area from critical habitat if he determines that the benefits of such exclusion outweigh the benefits of specifying such area as part of the critical habitat, unless he determines, based on the best scientific and commercial data available, that the failure to designate such are as critical habitat areas will result in the extinction of the species concerned.[12]

Therefore, although economic factors are not to be considered in the listing of a species as endangered or threatened, economic factors are considered in the designation of critical habitat, and some habitat areas may be excluded from designation based on such concerns, unless the failure to designate habitat would result in the extinction of the subject species.

Pre-listing Activities

The question may arise as to what the responsibilities of the Federal Government are toward a species that is proposed for listing but has not yet been listed. This question could be important because there may be a significant time between the proposal for listing and the actual listing, during which time a Federal agency could be faced with decisions on contracts and management actions of various types. Under current law, an agency must confer with the Secretary of the Interior on any agency action which is likely to jeopardize the continued existence of any species proposed to be listed or result in the destruction or adverse modification of critical habitat proposed to be designated for such species.[13] The implementing regulations state that the conference is designed to assist the Federal agency and an applicant in identifying and resolving potential conflicts at an early stage in the planning process.[14]

The *conference* process that applies to species that are proposed for listing is distinct from the *consultation* process that applies to listed species. The conference is intended to be less formal, and to permit the Fish and Wildlife Service to advise an agency on ways to minimize or avoid adverse effects. A Federal agency would have to follow more formal procedures and provide more

---

[12] 16 U.S.C. 1533(b)(2).
[13] 16 U.S.C. 1536 (a)(4).
[14] 16 U.S.C. 1536(a)(4).

complete documentation once a species is listed. However, the agency may choose to follow the more complete and formal processes even at the proposed listing state in order to avoid duplication of effort later.[15]

The ESA states that the conference stage does not require a limitation on the irreversible or irretrievable commitment of resources to an agency action which would foreclose reasonable and prudent alternative measures. However, once a species is listed an agency will have definite responsibilities, and an agency might consider it prudent at the proposed listing stage both to avoid harm to a precarious species and to avoid possible liability for compensation arising from agency actions creating private rights which later cannot be exercise. An agency might, for example, choose to avoid holding timber sales in an area containing a proposed species. Congress may wish to provide additional policy and guidelines for the proposed listing state.[16]

Post-listing Activities

The listing of a species as threatened or endangered triggers certain requirements and restrictions under section 7 of the ESA (16 U.S.C. 1536). All Federal agencies are required to consult with the Secretary about proposed actions; to utilize their authorities in furtherance of the act; and to insure that any action authorized, funded, or carried out by the agency is not likely to jeopardize the continued existence of any endangered species or threatened species, or result in the destruction or adverse modification of critical habitat unless the agency has been granted an exemption under the ESA.

EXEMPTIONS

The exemption process is the principal way in which economic factors are intended to be taken into account under the ESA. There have only been a few instances to date in which the exemption process was initiated, and only one in which an exemption was granted. Figure 1 shows the steps of the process, and the reader may wish to refer to it while proceeding through this part. Also, see

---

[15] *Id.*
[16] Section 1002 of Pub. L. No. 100-478, 102 Stat. 2306 requires the Secretary to implement a system to monitor effectively the status of "candidate" species (species with respect to which a finding has been made that a petition to list a species appears warranted, but as to which listing is precluded or no longer necessary) and to prevent a significant risk to the well being of any such species.

Appendices A, B, and C for chronologies and discussions of the five attempts to secure exemptions under the ESA.

As originally enacted, the ESA contained an absolute prohibition against activities detrimental to listed species. When the prospective impoundment of water behind the nearly completed Tellico dam threatened to eradicate the only known population of the snail darter (a fish related to perch), the Supreme Court concluded that the then current "plain language" of the ESA mandated that the gates of the dam not be closed.

> "Concededly, this view of the Act will produce results requiring the sacrifice of the anticipated benefits of the project and of many millions of dollars in public funds. But examination of the language, history, and structure of the legislation under review here indicates beyond doubt that Congress intended endangered species to be afforded the highest of priorities."[17]

After this Supreme Court decision, the ESA was amended to include a process by which economic impacts could be reviewed and projects exempted from the restrictions that otherwise would apply. As originally enacted, the exemption process involved a review board, but has been amended so that it is structured as follows.·

The "Endangered Species Committee" (ESC) reviews applications for exemptions. The ESC is composed of the Secretary of Agriculture, the Secretary of the Army, the Chairman of the Council of Economic Advisors, the Administrator of the Environmental Protection Agency, the Secretary of the Interior (who chairs the ESC),[18] the Administrator of the National Oceanic and Atmospheric Administration and one individual from each affected State. Committee members from the State collectively have one vote.[19]

Eligible Applicants

A Federal agency, the Governor of the State in which an agency action will occur, or a permit or license applicant may apply to the Secretary for an exemption for an agency action. How an agency action is structured—whether, for example, it is a separate action or a forest-wide program—could be relevant to the various findings required under the exemption procedures. The term "permit or license applicant" is defined in the ESA only as a person whose application to a

---

[17] Tennessee Valley Authority v. Hill, 437 U.S. 153, 174 (1978).
[18] 16 U.S.C. 1536(e).
[19] 50 CFR 453.05(d).

Federal agency for a permit or license has been denied primarily because of the application of the taking prohibitions to the agency action.[20] The regulations do not elaborate on who is included within this term.[21] Agency representatives have indicated that it includes neither a prospective timber purchaser nor a person who holds a current contract. Industry representative disagree on both of these points.

An exemption application form a Federal agency must describe the consultation process carried out between the head of the Federal agency and the Secretary, and include a statement explaining why the action cannot be altered or modified to conform with the requirements of the statue. All applications must be submitted to the Secretary not later than 90 days after completion of the consultation process if the applicant is a Federal agency, or 90 days from the final agency action if the applicant is a permit or a license applicant. An application must set out the reasons the applicant considers an exemption warranted. The Secretary then publishes a notice of receipt of the application in the Federal Register and notifies the Governor of each affected State (as determined by the Secretary) so that State members can be appointed to the ESC. The Secretary may deny the application if the preliminary steps have not been completed.

To be eligible for an exemption, the Federal agency concerned and the exemption applicant must have carried out the consultation processes required under section 7 of the ESA (16 U.S.C. 1536) in good faith. They also must have made a reasonable and responsible effort to develop and fairly consider modifications or reasonable and prudent alternatives to the proposed action that would not jeopardize the continued existence of any endangered or threatened species or result in the destruction or adverse modification of critical habitat of a species. In addition, they must have conducted required biological assessments; and, to the extent determinable within the time provided, refrained from making any irreversible or irretrievable commitment of resources that would foreclose the formulation or implementation of reasonable and prudent alternatives that would avoid jeopardizing the species and habitat. These qualifying requirements were put in place to insure that the exemption process is meaningful and that consideration of the issues would not be preempted by actions already taken.[22] Additional requirements for an application are contained in the relevant regulations.[23]

It is important to note that the exemption process begins only *after* a species is listed, consultation has occurred, a finding has been made that the agency is

---

[20] 16 U.S.C. 1532(12).
[21] 50 C.F.R. 450.01.
[22] 16 U.S.C. 1536(g).
[23] 50 C.F.R. 450 *et.seq.*

likely to jeopardize a species, and it is determined that there are no reasonable and prudent alternatives to the agency action.

Secretarial Review

The Secretary is to determine whether an application is qualified within 20 days or a time mutually agreeable to the applicant and the Secretary. Within 140 days of the time the Secretary determines that the applicant is qualified, the Secretary, the consultation with the other members of the ESC, must hold a formal hearing on the application and prepare a report. The purpose of the formal hearing is to collect evidence both favoring and opposing the exemption.[24] The Secretary's report reviews whether the applicant has made any irreversible or irretrievable commitment of resources; discusses the availability of reasonable and prudent alternatives and the benefits of each, provides a summary of the evidence concerning whether the action is the public interest and is nationally or regionally significant; and outlines appropriate and reasonable mitigation and enhancement measures which should e considered by the ESC.[25]

Committee Determination

Within 30 days after receiving the report of the Secretary, the ESC is to grant or deny an exemption. The ESC shall grant an exemption if, based on the evidence, the ESC determines that

(i)   there are no reasonable and prudent alternatives to the agency action;

(ii) the benefits of such action clearly outweigh the benefits of alternative courses of action consistent with conserving the species or its critical habitat, and such action is in the public interest;

(iii) the action is of regional or national significance; and

(iv) neither the federal agency concerned nor the exemption applicant made any irreversible or irretrievable commitment of resources prohibited by subsection (d) of this section [commitments as described above that jeopardize species or critical habitat].[26]

---

[24] H.R. Rep. No. 835, 97th Cong., 2d Sess. 28 (1982).
[25] 16 U.S.C. 1536(g)(5).
[26] 16 U.S.C. 1536(h)(1)(A).

Mitigation

If the ESC grants an exemption, it also must establish reasonable mitigation and enhancement measures that are "necessary and appropriate to minimize the adverse effects" of an approved action on the species or critical habitat.[27] The exemption applicant (whether Federal agency, Governor, or permit or license applicant) is responsible for carrying out and paying for mitigation.[28]

The costs of mitigation and enhancement measures specified in an approved exemption must be included in the overall costs of continuing the proposed action and the applicant must report annually to the Council on Environmental Quality on compliance with mitigation and enhancement measures.[29]

Review by Secretary of State

There are certain limits on the ESC's authority. For example, the ESC cannot grant an exemption for an agency action if the Secretary of State, after a hearing and a review of the proposed agency action, certifies in writing that carrying out the action would violate a treaty or other international obligation of the United States.[30] This provision is relevant because the spotted owl is listed[31] as a species protected under the Migratory Bird Treaty Act (MBTA),[32] which in turn implements the migratory bird treaties to which the United States is a party. The convention between the United States and Mexico ultimately resulted in the addition of two scientific Families of owls to the protection of that treaty.[33] Current regulations list the spotted owl (*Strix occidentalis*) as a protected migratory bird, without any distinction as to subspecies.[34]

As the ESA is currently written, the Secretary of State is to make this determination within 60 days "of any application made under this section", a time

---

[27] 16 U.S.C. 1536(h)(1)(B).
[28] 16 U.S.C. 1536(l)(1).
[29] 16 U.S.C. 1536(l)(2).
[30] 16 U.S.C. 1536(i), Other provisions not relevant to the spotted owl context require the Committee to grant an exemption if the Secretary of Defense finds that an exemption is necessary for reasons of national security. (16 U.S.C. 1536(j)), and permit the President to make exemption determinations in certain cases involving facilities in a disaster areas. (16 U.S.C. 1536(p)).
[31] 50 C.F.R. 10.13.
[32] Act of July 3, 1918, c. 128, 40 Stat. 755, codified at 16 U.S.C. 703 *et seq.*
[33] Convention for the Protection of Migratory Birds and Game Mammals, February 7, 1936, United States-Mexico, 50 Stat. 1311, T.S. No. 912.
[34] 50 C.F.R. 10.13. There are three subspecies of spotted owl, one of which inhabits areas on both sides of the border with Mexico. The northern spotted owl (*Strix occidentalis caurina*) does not migrate. The regulations do not distinguish between the subspecies.

limit which may be unrealistic given the longer length of time the Secretary of the Interior has to prepare the report that will fully describe the agency action to be reviewed by the Secretary of State.

Duration and Effect of Exemption

An exemption is permanent unless the Secretary finds that the exemption would result in the extinction of a species that was not the subject of consultation or was not identified in a biological assessment and the ESC determines that the exemption should not be permanent.[35]

The ESA expressly states that the penalties that normally apply to the taking of an endangered or threatened species do not apply to takings resulting from actions that are exempted.[36]

Interaction with Other Laws

The granting of an exemption from the penalties that otherwise would apply under the Endangered Species Act does not necessarily solve all of the problems arising from the destruction of spotted owls and their habitat. For example, the National Forest Management Act[37] requires the Forest Service to develop forest management plans that provide for diversity of plant and animal communities",[38] and current regulations under that act require that fish and wildlife habitat be managed to maintain viable populations of existing native vertebrate species in a forest planning area.[39]

Furthermore, criminal penalties apply to the taking of migratory birds under the Migratory Bird Treaty Act,[40] the act that implements the migratory bird treaties of the United States. As noted above, the spotted owl currently is listed as

---

[35] 16 U.S.C. 1536(h).
[36] 16 U.S.C. 1536(o).
[37] Public Law No. 94-588, 90 Stat, 2949, codified at 16 U.S.C. 1601 *et seq.*
[38] 16 U.S.C. 1604(g)(3)(B).
[39] 36 C.F.R. 219.9 For planning purposes, a viable population is "one which has the estimated numbers and distribution of reproductive individuals to insure its continued existence is well distributed in the planning area. In order to insure that viable populations will be maintained, habitat must be provided to support, at least, a minimum number of reproductive individuals and that habitat must be well distributed so that those individuals can interact with others in the planning area."
[40] Act of July 13, 1918, c. 128, 40 Stat. 755, codified at 16 U.S.C. 703-711.

a protected migratory bird. The penalties of the MBTA apply to non-federal persons, and may apply to Federal personnel as well.[41]

The ESA does not address how the exemption process relates to these other statutes.

Figure 1. A Flowchart of the Major Steps in Obtaining an Exemption

---

[41] This issue arose in connection with the killing of migratory birds as a result of contaminated water in the Kesterson Refuge in California. In a letter from F. Henry Habicht II, Assistant Attorney General to Hon. Marian Blank Horn, Principal Deputy Solicitor, dated October 7, 1985, the Department of Justice wrote that such decisions would be made on a case-by-case basis, but that In our view, the MBTA should not be construed to authorize prosecution of federal officials and employees who are engaged in congressionally authorized projects that result in incidental bird deaths, provided that (1) the officials act within the authority granted by Congress and the employees perform their job responsibilities with due car under the circumstances; and (2) they make a good faith attempt to comply, to the extent practicable under the circumstances, with the MBTA.

Notes on Figure 1.

This three-page figure is a guide to the issues brought up in the spotted owl and old growth controversy specifically. Consequently, some steps that could be important in other applications (e.g., special requirements if the exemption might involve national security issues) are omitted or condensed.

Box 10. There are three categories of eligible applicants: a Federal agency, a Governor, or a permit or license applicant. If the applicant is attempting to obtain a permit or license, the applicant must await final agency action before applying for an exemption. The Pittston case raised the issue of whether an appeal and an exemption could be pursued simultaneously, and Congress clarified the law on this process.

Box 11. A State nominates representatives, and the President selects one from the State's list. According to regulations, if three States are involved, . each representative has one-third of a vote.

Box 12. This issue could be important in the spotted owl controversy, since all North American owls are protected under the Migratory Bird Treaty Act and under a U.S.-Mexico Migratory Bird Treaty.

Box 16. Briefly, the Secretary's report must cover these issues: (a) any alternatives to the project that would still protect the owl and its habitat, and the benefits of these alternatives and of the proposed action; (b) evidence on the significance of the project and the public interest aspects of the Agency's action; (c) any mitigation or enhancement measures for the ESC to consider; and (d) whether the Agency and the applicant have avoided irretrievable commitment of resources that would foreclose on any of the alternatives to the project.

Box 17. The ESC is to make its determination base on four factors: (a) Is there a reasonable and prudent alternative to the project that would be consistent with conserving the species? (b) Do the benefits of the Agency action clearly outweigh the benefits of the alternatives, and is the proposal in the public interest? (c) Is the agency action regionally or nationally significant? (d) Have the Agency and the applicant avoided irretrievable commitment of resources that would foreclose alternatives consistent with conserving the species?

Box 19. These mitigation measures must be necessary and appropriate. The applicant must pay for these mitigation measures, but may contract with a Federal agency to carry them out on its behalf. Since the law makes no distinction among types of applicants, this provision would apply whether the applicant was a Federal agency, a Governor, or a permit or license applicant.

Conclusions

The Endangered Species Act is structured so that the basic decision to list a species as either threatened or endangered is to be based only on scientific information. Once that decision to list is made, however, economic factors are taken into account in two ways: in the designation of critical habitat of a listed species, and in the exemption procedure. However, there has been very little experience with the exemption process, perhaps because the consultation and negotiation stages, also provided for in the ESA, accomplish the purpose of modifying proposed actions early in the planning and development stages so as to avoid harm to listed species.

How the exemption process would work in the spotted owl context is problematic. Before the exemption process is reached an "agency action" must first be structured, there must be consultation and findings that the agency action is likely to jeopardize the continued existence of a listed species or result in the destruction or adverse modification of critical habitat of the species, and that there is no prudent or feasible alternative to the proposed agency action. Subsequently, the ESC would have to make all the required findings on which an exemption rests.

Furthermore, it is not clear how the granting of an exemption under the ESA relates to the duty to protect the spotted owl and its habitat under other laws. These issues was it the interpretation of the agencies or further action by Congress.

10 Frequently Asked Questions about the Endangered Species Act and Spotted Owls

1) *Can economic factors be considered under the ESA?* Under the 1982 amendments to the ESA, Congress made it very clear that "solely" scientific factor should be used in determining whether to list a species. The goal was to make the initial step purely one of determining whether a species needed the assistance of the law. *Only after listing* economic factors considered. In effect, the law asks two questions, in this order: (a) Is this species in trouble? (b) If the answer is "yes" and the species is listed, are there alternatives to harming the species, and do the costs of saving it exceed the benefits?

2) *Right now, FWS is considering a proposal to list the northern spotted owl as threatened throughout its range. Is FWS restricted to accepting or rejecting*

that proposal, or does it have other choices beyond the proposal? Under the ESA, *populations* of vertebrate species (animals with backbones) can be listed separately. Since most biologists agree that there are five populations of northern spotted owls it is possible that FWS could decide to list some, all, or none, as threatened or endangered. For example, FWS might decide to list the Olympic and Oregon Coast populations as endangered, the Washington and Oregon Cascade populations are threatened, and the Klamath population as unlisted. Other options are also possible.

3) *After a species is listed, when can economic factors be considered?* Economic factors can be considered in either of two stages: in the designation of critical habitat, or in an application for an exemption. As a practical matter, FWS and the National Marine Fisheries Service have often failed to designate critical habitat for many species, since the process is very costly, subject to much dispute, and is not the section of the law that offers the greatest protection to listed species anyway.

4) *Who is eligible to apply for an exemption?* A federal agency, the Governor(s) of an affected State(s), and a "permit or license applicant." The law and its regulations do not elaborate on who qualifies as a permit or license applicant.

5) *Is a timber company, for these purposes, considered a permit or license applicant if it wants to buy some timber in the future?* No, according to agency officials; yes, according to some industry spokespersons. *What about a company that has already purchased a timber contract, but hasn't cut it yet?* Here the situation is murky. Federal agency representatives assert that current contract holders are not eligible, either. But industry observers strongly disagree. (This question should not be confused with that of what compensation might be due to a current contract holder who is prevented from harvesting a sale because of the presence of newly listed spotted owls.)

6) *The law states that the ESC can require mitigation as a condition of granting an exemption. Who pays for that?* The applicant is responsible for carrying out and paying for any required mitigation measures. (The applicant may contract with a Federal agency to do the mitigation, but the applicant remains legally and financially responsible for it.) If the applicant promises to carry out mitigation and does not do so, the applicant is open to the civil and criminal penalties specified in the law. There has never been a case in which a Governor has applied for an exemption under ESA. Whether the Governor would pay for the exemption, or diverting current spending form other programs is unclear. The ESA is silent on *how* the Governor should pay, but only specifies that the Governor (when he/she is the applicant) must pay.

7) *How stiff can the mitigation requirements be?* The ESC may require any reasonable mitigation measures that are necessary and appropriate. In theory, these measures might include those described in agency management plans, the Report of the Interagency Scientific Committee, or any other possible options.

8) *In the spotted owl case specifically, what would the exemption application actually be for? A particular sale? An agency's entire timber sale program? Or something in between?* While there doesn't appear to be any legal barrier to using the exemption process on a sale by sale basis, as a practical matter this would probably not be attempted. The agency action could be an entire program. The need for documenting economic and biological factors may drive the off exemption sought. It might, for example, be impossible to meet the test of a national or regional impact in a single sale. The applicant has the burden of proof in showing that other alternatives (banning log exports, alternative economic development, or whatever) have been considered, and for one reason or another aren't reasonable or prudent. The *Federal Register* of Dec. 5, 1985, contains an instructive list of 15 project-specific questions that another exemption applicant was asked to answer in applying for an exemption. These questions make clear that alternatives that would be beyond the scope of the action agency to carry out on its own must be considered.

9) *Could an exemption be at an intermediate level-say, the timber program in a National Forest, a BLM district, or even in one of the five recognized populations of northern spotted owls?* Nothing like that has ever been attempted, but it may be possible. Note that the exemption would be for the specified program or activity as described in the application. If, for example the Forest Service applied for an exemption for its timber sales on the Siuslaw National Forest, and actually obtained it, the granting of the exemption would not mean that, say, a new low head hydroelectric project, a nearby housing development, or a new interstate highway in the same area would be exempt from the ESA's protections of the spotted owl or of any other species. In fact, such projects might be subject to even closer scrutiny as a result of the exemption.

10) *If an exemption were granted under ESA, would the applicant be insulated from all other laws which might protect the owls?* Not necessarily. For example, the Migratory Bird Treaty Act (MBTA) protects nearly all bird species in North America, including owls. Depending on the particular activity, it is conceivable that an applicant who had received an exemption could carry out the activity but then face charges of violating the MBTA. Such a violation could carry criminal penalties. The ESA contains a provision

which forbids the granting of an exemption in the first place if the Secretary of State certifies that the activity as proposed would violate an international treaty. Moreover, other laws, such as the National Forest Management Act, or the National Environmental Policy Act might still apply. The interaction of the ESA exemption process with other laws is not clear.

APPENDIX A: A CHRONOLOGY OF GRAYBACKS

ISSUE: The Platte River, in its lower reaches in Nebraska, is a major stopover site in the whooping cranes' mitigation between southern Texas and north central Canada. FWA determined that the construction of the Grayrocks Dam and Reservoir in Wyoming, along with existing projects in the Platte River basin, would have jeopardized the downstream habitat of whooping cranes. Specifically, a reduction in instream flow as a consequence of the project as originally designed could have damaged the cranes' resting sites. (The reduction in the total flow would also have threatened Nebraska irrigation interests.)

Chronology

Date	Event
1976	Lawsuits (*Nebraska v. REA* and *Nebraska v. Ray*—later consolidates as one case) are filed by the State of Nebraska, the National Audubon Society, and the National Wildlife Federation against the Corps of Engineers and against the Rural Electrification Administration (REA). The suits allege a failure to consult with the FWS under section 7 of ESA, and a possible violation of NEPA.
12/76	The REA grants a loan guarantee to the Basin Electric Power Cooperative for construction of Grayrocks dam.
10/77	Army Corps of Engineers (COE) requests Sec. 7 consultation with FWS. FWS initially replies that a 3 year study is necessary before it can offer a biological opinion on the effects of the project.
03/78	COE issues a Section 404 dredge and fill permit under the Clean Water Act.
05/15/78	FWS designates certain parts of the Platte River as critical habitat for whooping cranes.
07/19/78	Senate passes ESA reauthorization; bill contains an exemption process, which creates an Endangered Species Committee (ESC), but no specific exemption of Tellico or Grayrocks.
09/30/78	Scheduled expiration of ESA authorization.

10/78	Federal district court finds COE and REA in violation of Sec. 7 of ESA. The case is appealed to the 8th Circuit, which stays a lower court injunction.
10/14/78	House passes ESA reauthorization; bill contains language with an exemption process, and specific language affecting Tellico and Grayrocks.
10/14/78	House and Senate pass ESA conference report for S. 2899. Provisions on Tellico and Grayrocks require that (1) the ESC meet within 30 days of enactment; (2) exemption must be granted if stated provisions are satisfied; (3) decision must be made within 90 days of enactment, or the projects will be automatically exempted. A separate provision, recognizing the possibility of a settlement in the Grayrocks case, states that if FWS renders a biological opinion that the project as then planned would jeopardize the cranes, then REA, DOI, and the Corps must require modifications to insure that the Grayrocks project does not jeopardize the continue existence of endangered species (i.e., whooping cranes).
11/10/78	President Carter, despite encouragement from DOI for a veto, signs ESA reauthorization (P.L. 05-632).
11/78	FWS concludes that Grayrocks project would jeopardize the survival of whooping cranes. (Note: the date of this opinion is uncertain, but it is *after* 11/10/78).
12/04/78	Parties to *Nebraska v. REA* reach a settlement which would place constraints on operation of the Grayrocks Reservoir and establish a permanent, irrevocable trust fund of $7.5 million for maintenance of the cranes' critical habitat. But before agreement is finalized, parties agree that 3 conditions must be met: 1. DOI must concur that he implemented agreement and completed project would satisfy the requirements of ESA. 2. Either the project gets an exemption from ESA or the ESC determines that no exemption is needed. 3. The Federal appeals court must dismiss the litigation with prejudice (i.e., the plaintiffs cannot file the same suit unless the agreement has been violated).
12/08/78	ESC meets to consider exemption.
12/08/78	FWS issues biological opinion on the effects of the Grayrocks project.
01/08/79	Simultaneous hearings in Cheyenne, WY, and Washington, DC, on exemption proposal.
01/10/79	Deadline for any comments for record for ESC deliberations.
01/19/79	Staff Report is ESC is issued for their use as background in determining whether to grant an exemption.

01/23/79	ESC grants exemption for Grayrocks Dam and Reservoir by unanimous vote. Decision includes specified mitigation measures which included: (1) limiting maximum annual water use to 23,250 acre-feet/year; (2) making certain releases of water at critical times of year; (3) replacing water withdrawn in an irrigation project in the Platte River watershed; (4) creating a permanent trust fund of $7.5 million for maintenance and enhancement of critical whooping crane habitat on the Platte River; and (5) other specified measures. The exemption is granted on the condition that mitigation and enhancement features are funded concurrently with the rest of the project, paid for by the project, and carried out without regard to the final settlement and compromise signed by the litigants in *Nebraska v. REA* and *Nebraska v. Ray.*
02/08/79	If no decision had been made by ESC before this date, the Grayrocks project would have been automatically exempted.

APPENDIX B: A CHRONOLOGY OF TELLICO

ISSUE: A dam on the Little Tennessee was proposed for its navigation, power, and economic benefits. Opposition to the project arose early, due to concern over fishing, recreation, Native American religious sites, and loss of agricultural land. After discovery of the snail darter, project opponents had to decide whether to abandon their old arguments and pin their hopes on a small fish. According to one observer, "opponents would have preferred a weapon like a bald eagle or a bear or a buffalo. But what they had was [a] fish."[42]

Chronology

Date	Event
1936	A dam on the Little Tennessee River, to improve navigation and generate electricity, is first proposed by TVA.
1963	Now named the Tellico Project, TVA again proposes the dam. Acquisition of additional lands is included, in order to provide for industrial, commercial, and residential development. The cost of the revised project is estimated at $41 million.
1966	Tellico project is authorized.

---

[42] p. 189 *in* William B. Wheeler and Michael J. McDonald, *TVA and the Tellico Dam.* University of Tennessee Press. Knoxville. 1986. 290 p.

1967	First annual appropriation for the project is passed. (Money is appropriated for each year thereafter.)
1971	Lawsuit filed, contending that Tellico's EIS was inadequate and violated NEPA. (Note: the 1973 ESA had not become a Federal law at this point.)
08/12/73	Dr. David Etnier of the University of Tennessee discovers snail darters in the stretch of the Little Tennessee that would be impounded by Tellico; he realizes that the fish is a species new to science.
10/09/75	Snail darter is listed an endangered under ESA.
02/18/76	*Hill v. TVA* filed; plaintiffs argue that Tellico violated ESA.
10/12/76	FWS issues biological opinion that Tellico, as proposed, would jeopardize the continued existence of the snail darter.
04/76	District court dismisses the cases on the merits; plaintiffs appeal, and the 6th Circuit issues an injunction preventing closure of the dam, but allowing construction to continue.
01/31/77	Appellate Court holds that ESA does apply to Tellico. It grants an injunction that stops the remaining 10% of construction except for structures that would be required even if project is never completed. TVA appeals to Supreme Court.
06/15/78	Supreme Court affirms decision of Appellate Court.
07/19/78	Senate passes ESA reauthorization; bill contains an exemption process, which creates an Endangered Species Committee (ESC), but no specific exemption for Tellico and Grayrocks.
09/30/78	Scheduled expiration of ESA authorization.
10/14/78	House passes ESA reauthorization; bill contains language with an exemption process, and specific language directing an expedited procedure for Tellico and Grayrocks.
10/14/78	House and Senate pass ESA conference report for S. 2899. Provisions on Tellico and Grayrocks require that (1) the ESC meet within 30 days of enactment; (2) exemption must be granted if stated provisions are satisfied; (3) decision must be made within 90 days of enactment, or the projects will be automatically exempted.
11/10/78	President Carter, despite encouragement from DOI for a veto, signs ESA reauthorization (P.L. 95-632).
12/08/78	ESC meets to consider exemption.
01/08/79	Hearings held in Knoxville, TN, and Washington, DC, on proposal for exemption.
01/10/79	Deadline for any comments for record for ESC deliberations.
01/19/79	Staff Report to ESC is issued for their use as background in determining whether to grant an exemption.

01/23/79	ESC rejects exemption for Tellico. The Chair of the ESC, Interior Secretary Cecil Andrus, states "Frankly, I hate to see the snail darter get the credit for stopping a project that was ill-conceived and uneconomical in the first place."
02/07/79	An ex officio Chairman of the ESC, Cecil Andrus signs the decision denying the exemption for Tellico.
02/08/79	If no decision had been made by ESC before this date, the Tellico Project would have been automatically exempted.
06/18/79	Rep. John Duncan (TN) offers amendment to H.R. 4388 (Energy and Water Appropriations for FY80), exempting Tellico from ESA and other laws; the House accepts the language on voice vote, with little discussion.
07/17/79	Senate passes an amendment (53 yeas to 45 nays; roll call vote #180) to strike House language exempting Tellico from the requirements of ESA and from other laws. (A vote of "yea" was a vote in favor of the fish, farmers, and Indians; a vote of "nay" was a vote to finish the dam, exempt it from ESA, and proceed with development.)
09/10/79	The Senate recedes from its earlier amendment of 7/17, and agrees to the conference language which exempts Tellico from ESA as well as other laws. The vote is 48 "yeas" to 44 "nays"; a vote of "yea" is a vote for the dam and development; a vote of "nay" is a vote for the fish, farmers, and Indians (roll call vote #269).
09/25/79	President Carter signs the Energy and Water Development Appropriations (H.R. 4388, P.L. 96-69), expressing regret at doing so.
11/29/79	Workers at Tellico close the gates on the dam, allowing filling of the reservoir to begin.
07/05/84	FWS reclassifies snail darter as threatened, rather than endangered, based largely on new data on the distribution f the species. The notice also rescinds the designation of the Tellico Dam area as critical habitat, since the species no longer exists in that area. At the time of the notice, the fish were known from small populations at 9 locations in the Tennessee River watershed.

APPENDIX C: THREE ATTEMPTS AT AN EXEMPTION

Pittston Refinery, Eastport, Maine

The Pittston Company wished to build an oil refinery at Eastport, Maine, in the mouth of the Bay of Fundy, an area with one of the world's greatest tidal fluctuations (over 20 feet). In their biological opinions, FWS held that the refinery would jeopardize bald eagles, and the National Marine Fisheries Service (NMFS), which has jurisdiction over most marine species, held that the project would endanger whales. Initially, EPA denied Pittston's application for a permit to discharge effluent. The company responded with two actions in 1979. First, it administratively appealed the denial. Second, it applied for an exemption under ESA. The company felt it was forced to take the two actions simultaneously because the ESA required an application for exemption to be filed within 90 days of the denial of a permit. In January, 1979, the various parties agreed to suspend the exemption process while a compromise was sought. The effort at compromise was unsuccessful.

Environmental groups sued, asking an injunction to stop the application for the exemption.[43] They argued that the case was brought prematurely, before the issue had finished with the administrative appeals process. In effect, they argued that the ESA itself was poorly written, in that it forced the applicant to carry out two procedures (appeal and exemption) simultaneously. The U.S. Justice Department agreed that the law was poorly written, and that the exemption process should not run concurrently with an appeal.

This confusion, and apparent conflict, was addressed by Congress in the 1982 amendments to ESA. These amendments clarified that the exemption process was to be invoked only after the issuance of a final biological opinion, and after other means of compliance had failed. In the case of a permit or license, the exemption process must also wait until after an agency formally denies the permit or license. (16 U.S.C. 1536(g)(2)). The applicant may not simultaneously seek an administrative appeal and an exemption. The court eventually agreed that the exemption process could not begin until the appeals process was finished.[44]

Consolidated Grain and Barge Company, Illinois

This company (CGBC) sought to build a docking area for barges at Mound City, IL, on the Ohio River. The area was habitat for the endangered *Plethobasus*

---

[43] *See*, Pittston Company v. Endangered Species Committee, 14 ERC 1257, 10 ELR 20248 (D.D.C., 1980). The court commented that:
The exemption process was designed to resolve endangered species conflicts after other administrative remedies, including consultation have been exhausted. It makes no sense to initiate an exemption process before it has been determined that there is a need for an exemption in the first place. This provision insures exemption applications will be filed, in cases involving permit or license applicants, when the application is ripe for review.

[44] Since that time, "the issue just disappeared, because Pittston gave up", in the words of one DOI observer.

cooperianus (Orange-footed pearly mussel). FWS issued a negative biological opinion to the Army Corps of Engineers (COE), which on that basis denied the permit. Initially, the owner of the property agreed to provide funds for the exemption application, although CGBC was not willing to commit similar funds. On Nov. 6, 1985, FWS published a notice of the application in the *Federal Register*.

On Dec. 6, 1985, the FWS published a *Federal Register* notice[45] of a hearing on Jan. 28, 1986, to be held in St. Louis. The notice indicated that the DOI Secretary agreed that the threshold criteria for calling for the exemption had been met, and set the details for the next stage of the process, i. e., the hearing. The FT notice also reminded interested parties that the applicant had the burden of proof in the proceedings.

At a pre-hearing conference with an Administrative Law Judge on Jan. 8, 1986, CGBC sent no one to represent its interest. A partner in a law firm of the lawyer who was hired by the landowner was present, but said he had limited information concerning the issue, and had no list of witness which CGBC would call. The lawyer asked for a one week extension of the hearing, but before it was held, the application was withdrawn.

Suwanee River Authority, Florida

On July 30, 1986, the consulting engineer of the Suwanee River Authority (SRA) applied for an exemption from the Endangered Species Act regarding a project to dredge Alligator Pass in Suwanee Sound, Florida. It appears that the consulting engineer lacked authority from the SRA to apply on its behalf. The area provided habitat for the endangered manatee. The project needed a permit from COE, which denied it, primarily on the grounds of the presence of manatees.

On August 12, 1986, the board of the SRA refused to ratify the actions of its engineer, and asked that the application be withdrawn. In a letter on his own stationary, the engineer asked that the application be continued. After a further exchange of contradictory letters, the withdrawal still stood.

---

[45] The notice included a list of 15 specific questions addressed to CGBC that illustrated the types of specific information that would be sought for the record at the hearing. These questions could be very helpful for those seeking a guide to the details of an exemption application.

Chapter 4

ENDANGERED SPECIES ACT AMENDMENTS: ANALYSIS OF S. 1180 AND H.R. 2351

Pamela Baldwin and M. Lynne Corn

INTRODUCTION AND BACKGROUND

Because of wide-spread interest in possible amendments to the Endangered Species Act of 1973 (ESA),[1] there have been numerous requests for an analysis and critique of S. 1180 and H.R. 2351. H.R. 2351 was introduced on July 31, 1997, and S. 1180 on September 16, 1997. This report analyzes those bills. Each bill is discussed under various topic headings; the Senate bill will be described first, since it has been reported. Each section of the report describes briefly the current provisions of the ESA as it relates to that section.

Both the House and Senate bills focus on the process for listing declining species, developing recovery plans, and on new approaches to the problem of conserving habitat. The Senate bill would provide financial assistance to landowners and a separate bill (S. 1181) would provide tax incentives. The House bill does not provide direct financial assistance to landowners, but does contain tax incentives. The report will not address the tax provisions of H.R. 2351 at length. Neither bill would provide additional takings compensations for landowners above that required under the Constitution, and neither bill would provide special provisions related to the National Environmental Policy Act.

---

[1] Pub. L. No. 93-205, 87 Stat. 884, codified at 16 U.S.C. §§ 1531-1544.

The ESA has been one of the most controversial of all environmental laws, a fact that undoubtedly reflects the strict substantive provisions of this law. As a result of the ESA's standards, the Act often plays a role in disputes in which all sides agree that a given species is not the center of the debate.

The 1973 ESA began as a comprehensive attempt to protect all species and has evolved further to consider habitat protection as an integral part of that effort. It is administered primarily by the Secretary of the Interior through the Fish and Wildlife Service (FWS), but also by the Secretary of Commerce through the National marine Fisheries Service (NMFS) for certain marine species. Under the ESA, certain species of plants and animals (both vertebrate and invertebrate) are listed as either "endangered" or "threatened" according to assessments of the risk of their extinction. Once a species is listed, powerful legal tools are available to aid the recovery of the species and the protection of its habitat. As of January 31, 1998, 1,696 species of animals and plants (of which 1,126 occur in the United States and its territories) had been listed as either endangered or threatened. FO the U.S. listings, 744 were covered in 478 recovery plans. The authorization for funding under the ESA expired on October 1, 1992, but Congress has appropriated funds in each succeeding fiscal year. (See the FWS website at http://www.fws.gov/~r9endspp/html for further details. Also see Appendices I and II for an overview of the major domestic and international provisions of the current Act.)

LISTING

Under the definition of "species" in current law, any species or subspecies of plant or animal can be considered for addition to the lists of threatened or endangered species. In addition, only with respect to vertebrates (fish, amphibians, reptiles, birds, and mammals), distinct population segments may also be listed (*e.g.* populations of salmon that inhabit particular rivers). There were 207 candidate species and 99 proposed species awaiting listing decisions as of September 19, 1997.[2]

S. 1180

To the current factors (such as habitat loss, disease, predation, overuse, etc.) which may cause a species to be listed, S. 1180 (§2(c), p. 86) would add

---

[2] *See* 62 FED.REG. 49398-49411.

introduced species and competition. While these risk factors are almost certainly covered under the broad provisions of current law in §4(a)(1), their inclusion would emphasize them and could give agencies more options to respond to these threats. Introduced species may represent a serious economic threat to various sectors of the U.S. economy, which could use this addition as another legal tool to address the problem. Introduced species are particularly serious problems in certain areas, such as Hawaii, Guam, and Florida, and in agricultural grassland habitats. H.R. 2351 has no similar provision.

Backlog and Candidate Species
S. 1180 has no provision dealing specifically with the listing backlog, through its more extensive measures required for new listings would require increased appropriations if the current backlog is not to increase. S 1180 (§9(a), p. 170, inserting a new §3(2)) would define the term "candidate species" (not currently defined in ESA) to match current policy.

Contents of Petitions
Under current law, the Secretary jut merely determine that petitions to add, subtract, or modify the listing of a species are "substantive," after which the agency (FWS or NMFS) initiates its own full-scale review of the status of the species, requesting comments from all who wish to submit them. S. 1180 (§2(c)(4), p. 87-94, amending ESA's §4(b)(3)) would require documentation that the subject of the petition is a species, as defined in ESA; a description of specified available data on its range; an "appraisal" of available data on its status, trends, and threats; and an indication of what part of the information in the petition has been peer-reviewed or field-tested.

Data Standards
S. 1180 would retain the provision of current law that only the "best scientific and commercial data available" may be considered in a listing determination, but would specify I (in §2(a), p. 86, amending §3 to add a subsection (b)) that the Secretary must "give greater weight to scientific or commercial data that is empirical or has been field-tested or peer-reviewed." The committee report indicates that this language is meant to direct the Secretary when faced with "comparable" data to give greater weight to that which has been field-tested or peer reviewed.[3]

---

[3] S. Rep. 105-128 at 13 (1997).

Debates have occurred in the past over the use of scientific models in implementing ESA, particularly for making listing determinations. However, ESA requires federal agencies, especially FWS and NMFS, to make predictions about future events (*e.g.,* recovery, extinction, jeopardy, and survival). Presumably, since prediction without models could lapse into mere guesswork, this new standard may be intended to apply to the quality of data (and necessarily to the associated models), without actually precluding the use of models themselves. The intention of the proposed language, however, is not clear.

State Participation

Under current law, the Secretary must take into account any efforts being made by states to protect a species. The Secretary must also give notice to any affected states, and invite the comments of the relevant state agency and local jurisdictions, not less than 90 days before the effective date of the proposed regulation. S. 1180 (§ 102(c)(4), p. 89) would drop the requirement of notification of state governments regarding petitions deemed to meet the new criteria for petitions in the bill. (Current law requires only *Federal Register* give notice at this stage of the listing process.) The bill would require the Secretary to consider state assessments submitted during the comment period on the proposed regulation.

H.R. 2351

Section 2 (5) of the bill states as a finding that federal agencies and others should act to protect declining species before they need the full application of the ESA. Section 101 (p.6) would amend the definition of "species" (§3(16)) to permit the listing of populations of invertebrates and plants, if they represent the last remaining population in the United States of a particular species. Currently, only vertebrates may be listed at the population level.

Backlog and Candidate Species

Under current law, the term "candidate species" is not formally defined, but in practice it means those species on which a petition to list as been received, *and* for which the Service has on file sufficient information on biological vulnerability and threat(s) to support issuance of a proposed rule to list, but when issuance of the proposed rule is precluded by work on other species.[4] H.R. 2351 (§ 101, p. 6)

---

[4] The majority of species now listed were not the subjects of petitions, but were listed at the initiative of FWS, perhaps at the informal suggestion of other agencies. Processes for listing are largely the same as those for petitioned species ,but the deadlines of the petition process do not apply.

would define the term as new §3 (22) to include those that under current practice have been considered as candidate species and those for which a listing proposal may be appropriate based on available information, but for which further information is required to support a proposed rule. Like S. 1180 (which follows current policy), H.R. 2351 would not attach the term specifically to the petition process, leaving open the question of how it might apply to species now being considered for listing by the FWS. It is not clear at what stage specifically a species could be deemed to be "considered" by FWS. If it is the subject of a petition, the issue is clearer, but if troubling data on the species has merely come to the attention of a FWS biologist, would it be a considered species at that point, or would some higher level of attention and information be essential?

The bill (§p.11) would amend §4(b)(3)(C) of the Act to require a decision on listing within a year of enactment on petitions concerning al species previously determined to warrant listing, and within 4 years on any species judged to warrant listing after the date of enactment. Current law also contains deadlines for listing, but resources have proven inadequate to keep up with the number of proposed species. Without additional funding, it is unclear how further deadlines would help eliminate the backlog across the board, though they could provide a legal spur to action for particular species.

Contents of Petitions

H.R. 2351 (§104, p. 5) would add a new §4(b)(3)(E) to require petitioners to submit certain specified additional information on the species' range, population levels, and threats, and a bibliography of relevant information "to the maximum extent practicable." The latter condition was probably included to address that fact that such things as a species' historic range may not be known.

State and Tribal Participation

Under current law, the Secretary must take into account any efforts being made by states to protect a species. The Secretary must also give notice to any affected states, and invite the comments of the relevant state agency and local jurisdictions not less than 90 days before the effective date of the proposed regulation. H.R. 2351 would not change this procedure.

H.R. 2351 (§106, p. 16, amending §§6(c) and (d)) would include "any Indian tribe" for the purposes of participation in cooperative endangered species agreements. The term is not further defined. Some Indian tribes are federally recognized and others are not. It seems likely that at least recognized tribes are intended to be eligible, since these are more likely to control lands and waters and to have fish or wildlife departments able to manage such a program. It is not clear whether other entities such as Alaska Native Corporations, Hawaiian natives, etc., are also intended to be included.

DE-LISTING, DOWN-LISTING, AND UP-LISTING

Current Law

Under current law, the processes of de-listing a species, or changing its status from endangered to threatened ("down-listing"), or vice-versa ("up-listing"),are the same as those for listing a species. Any of these four processes faces the same requirements for information in petitions, and the same deadlines and options for hearings and public comment. In all four cases, FWS or NMFS may initiate the process. In all four cases, there are options for citizens to sue.

S. 1180

S. 1180 (§2(c)(3) and (4) would create new criteria for initiation of these processes. Subsection (3) (p. 87) would explicitly require the Secretary to initiate a de-listing determination if it were determined that the goals of the recovery plan had been met. Subsection (4) of S. 1180 would replace current § 4(b)(3).[5] It would include a new § 4(b)(3)(B) (p. 90) on petitions to up-list, down-list, or de-list a species currently on the ESA list, in contrast to petitions to add new species to the lists. Petitions for these three actions would apparently require the minimum documentation and deadlines specified under current law. However, S. 1180 would clarify the bases on which petitioners might request up-listing, down-listing, and de-listing. Petitions on any of the three could be based on a change in the factors that caused the species to be listed. Petitions to de-list only could be based on new data or re-interpretation of existing data, extinction, or attainment of the goals of the recovery plan.

---

[5] This lengthy subsection of the current law covers the timing of responses to petitions to change the list, the options for responding to a listing petition, the reviewability of negative decisions on listing, monitoring of candidate species, responses to petitions to change designated critical habitat, and other matters.

H.R. 2351

H.R. 2351 would make no changes that apply exclusively to de-listing, down-listing or up-listing.

THE ROLE OF SCIENCE

Property rights advocates, business interests, environmentalists, scientific organizations, and federal agencies have all decried, at various times, the inadequacy of the scientific basis of ESA decision-making. This unanimity is misleading, however, since the reasoning of the groups may be diametrically opposed. To some extent, this debate is predictable, given the lack of complete information on almost any wild species, and particularly given the even higher likelihood of poor data on rare species. If a species' distribution is poorly known (*e.g.,* Alabama sturgeon), should it be listed? If its taxonomic states (*e.g.* the northern goshawks of the Rocky Mountain area) is a matter of dispute, shout it be protected as a "distinct population segment"? If a species is wide-ranging, and begins to reappear in an area it once occupied (*e.g.,* wolves in Yellowstone), should these animals be regard as a "resident population"? Should a formerly widely-distributed species (*e.g.,* some salmon species) warrant protection in parts of its range, when it is still fairly abundant in other parts of its range? Should a species that is possibly "contaminated" with genes from other populations (*e.g.,* Florida panthers) warrant protection? More broadly, how should the federal government regulate in the (seemingly inevitable) absence of complete information, or navigate through a sea of gray areas?

People who face job loss or communities fearing economic instability would probably respond that the federal government should be quite certain that the species is present, is validly distinct, is protected over no wider an area than necessary, and is de-listed as soon as possible. Representatives of many scientific or environmental organizations would probably argue that the federal government should provide a margin of safety to recognize both the irreversibility of extinction and the frequent lack of complete information, should begin to protect species when their populations are still sufficient to avoid draconian measures (*e.g.,* whooping cranes, Pacific salmon, Florida panthers, *etc.*), and should seek to restore ecological balances wherever possible.

At this philosophical level, the "scientific" question becomes more one of law and policy than of science: how should regulations be administered and on which side should the burden of proof lie for protection? The information on which a decision is based may be quite acceptable on a purely scientific standpoint, but the resulting decision may still result in various parties criticizing the decision as "bad science"—for precisely opposite reasons.

In the current ESA, science is given absolute primacy in only one area: species may be listed "...solely on the basis of the best scientific and commercial data available..." However, in the remainder of the ESA, factors besides science may be considered, subject to certain restrictions such as avoiding jeopardy, a take of a member of a species, or adverse modification of critical habitat. A recovery plan, for example, must credibly lead to recovery of the species. But if various recovery options could all lead to that result, then the strategy with least economic impact may be chosen.

S.1180

Science in Listing Process

Under current law, when a petition is submitted, the Secretary must merely determine that it is "substantive." Under S. 1180 (§2(c)(4)(ii), p.88), considerably more data (see section on *Listing* for specifics) would be required of those petitioning to list, de-list, or down-list, or up-list a species. For those species already on the list, the required data may be fairly readily available. For petitions to list a species for the first time, the gathering of this information may prove a formidable obstacle.

In the next stage, under currently law, the Secretary must review available data. If the Secretary issues a proposed rule, there is opportunity for a hearing and oral and written public comment. S. 1180 (§2(c)(8), p. 97, adding a new §4(b)(10)) would also require that all listing proposals undergo peer review. Reviewers, to be selected from lists submitted by the National Academy of Sciences (NAS), would be required to meet several criteria (relating to expertise and conflict of interest) for selection.

For most vertebrates, sufficient, persons fulfilling the criteria might be readily available. For some obscure groups of organisms (*e.g.,* freshwater clams, freshwater fishes, and many insects), it may prove difficult to find enough people both to write the recovery plan, and to provide peer review for listing. It is not clear how this provision would be accomplished if there are insufficient experts. Also, neither bill addresses compensation of the scientists participating in peer review. Currently, academic scientists reviewing documents for their eligibility for grants or for publication, receive little, if any, compensation. Reviews are generally accomplished by mail, and are normally anonymous. The practical difficulties of grafting such a system onto a contentious area that may require extensive meetings, lost time from primary research and teaching activities, and potentially the polar opposite of academic anonymity are not well addressed in either bill.

Request for More Data

S. 1180 (§2(c)(8), p. 97, adding a new §(b)(9)) would require a special notice in the *Federal Register* when a listing proposal is published. The Secretary must describe "additional scientific and commercial data that would assist in the preparation of the recovery plan" and "the steps that the Secretary plans to take for acquiring additional data." The new subsection also says that these requirements do not waive or extend "any deadline for publishing a final rule to implement a determination..." The subsection appears to assume that such data could be obtained. It is unclear how a listing decision would be influenced if the additional data cannot, for whatever reason, be acquired in the allotted time.[6] At the time of a listing decision, it may not be known that the information for the recovery plan cannot be obtained. H. R. 2351 has no similar provision.

Science in the Recovery Process

Under current law, recovery team members must merely be "qualified." The actual plan itself has no required specific input from scientists, as opposed to any other group that may be interested in the plan.

Under S. 1180 (§3(b), p. 106, adding a new §5A(d)), members of the recovery team would be chosen "for their knowledge of the species or for their expertise in the elements of the recovery plan or its implementation." S. 1180 (§3(b), p. 109, adding a new §5A(e)(1)) also would require that a subset of the recovery team (those "with relevant scientific expertise") must "submit to the Secretary a recommended biological recovery goal to conserve and recover the species."

H.R. 2351

Science in Listing Process

Like S. 1180, H.R. 2351 (§104, p. 5, amending §(b)(3)) would require the petitioner to provide a broadly overlapping set of information, more detailed than current law requires, but only "to the maximum extent practicable." The phrase

---

[6] Such problems may readily arise if the species is active or present in the United States only part of the year; if the species is not found in this country; if crucial times for the relevant research are hampered by poor weather or damaged equipment; if funding is not available; or if relevant researchers have other obligations, to name a few predictable problems.

maybe helpful in instances when some, but not all, desirable information is available.

Science in the Recovery Process

Under H.R. 2351 (§105, p. 6, amending §4(f)) the Secretary would be required, in consultation with the National Academy of Sciences (NAS), to select independent scientists with expertise in the area, to determine the criteria that must be met for de-listing.

RECOVERY PLANS

Current Law

Under current law, recovery plans are to be developed for endangered and threatened species unless the Secretary finds that a plan will not promote the conservation of the species. The Secretary is to give priority to species that are most likely to benefit from such plans, particularly those species that are, or may be, in conflict with construction or other development projects or other forms of economic activity. A plan must include: 1) a description of site-specific management actions that are necessary to achieve the plan's goal; 2) objective, measurable criteria which, when met, would result in a determination that the species no longer needs the protections of the Act and can be removed from the lists; and 3) estimates of the time and costs required to carry out the plan and to achieve intermediate steps toward the goal. Current recovery plans have been interpreted as advisory rather than regulatory documents.

The Secretary may use the services of public and private agencies, institutions and "qualified persons" in developing recovery plans. Recovery teams are not subject to the Federal Advisory Committee Act (FACA).[7] The public is given notice and an opportunity to comment on recovery plans or revisions.

S. 1180

Section 3 of S. 1180 (pp. 104-130) would expand significantly on current provisions relating to recovery plans and §3(b) of the bill (p. 104) would establish a new, detailed §5 in the ESA devoted to that topic. (Current §5 of the Act on land acquisitions would become §5A.)

---

[7] 5 U.S.C. App. §§ 1-14.

When Required

Although recovery plans generally would be required, broader exceptions than are available under current law would be allowed. Recovery plans would be required for endangered species and threatened species that are indigenous to the United States or in waters with respect to which the United States exercises sovereign rights or jurisdiction.[8]

Under S. 1180, a recovery plan would not be required in every instance. Under new § 5(a) (p.104), the current exception for when the Secretary finds a plan would not promote the conservation of the species would be preserved. In addition, a recovery plan would not need to be prepared if there is an "existing plan or strategy" to conserve a species that is the "functional equivalent" of a recovery plan. It is not clear what would be regarded as an adequate functional equivalent, or whether an equivalent plan or strategy must contain all the elements otherwise specified for recovery plans by the bill, such as measurable goals that constitute recovery, etc.[9] The Secretary could specify details in implementing regulations. Given the absence of legislated guidance, it is possible that general agency planning documents might be deemed functional equivalents. The Secretary may also authorize a state agency to develop a recovery plan.

A new ESA § 18(e) (p. 129-130) would be added to require the phased-in preparation of recovery plans for *all* species listed before the amendments that would be made by the bill. Therefore, it appears that all species listed before enactment of the amendments would have recovery plans prepared, but not all species listed after enactment of the amendments would.

Scientific Basis Required

Recovery plans would be required to be based on "the best scientific and commercial data available" and to set out biological recovery goals to recover the species. These goals would be based *solely* on the best scientific and commercial data available and would e expressed as objective and measurable biological criteria, the achievement of which would result in de-listing.

Priorities

A system of priorities would be established in new § 5(b) (pp. 104-105) for developing recovery plans. The priority provisions in the bill are similar to the

---

[8] The Senate Report indicates that this would mean those waters landward of the outer boundary of the Exclusive Economic Zone established by Presidential Proclamation No. 5030, dated March 10, 1983. S. Rep 105-128 at 19 (1997).

[9] The Senate Report states that "only plans or strategies that have undergone similar procedural substantive requirements could serve as functional equivalents." *Id.*, at 19.

existing priorities, but would be expanded to include taxonomically distinct species, candidate species, and potential military conflicts as elements affecting priority status. Therefore, priority would be given to plans that address species facing immediate threats, multiple species, candidate species dependent on the same habitat as listed species, and plans that have the greatest likelihood of achieving recovery or those that would reduce conflicts with private property, jobs, other economic activities, and military training and operations. Since the recovery goals are to be based on science, the reduction of conflicts referred to here may mean reduction of conflicts through the certainty that recovery planning would provide. It is unclear what the priority to be given species that are "more taxonomically distinct" would mean in instances where the number of individuals of a species is ample in part of its range, but low in another part of its historic range. This was true, for example, with respect to the bald eagle that was plentiful in Alaska, but endangered in the lower 48 states. The eagle was listed as endangered in the lower states and has now recovered to the extent of being listed as threatened. Similar conditions also pertain to other species, such as the marbled murrelet. Under the bill language, it is possible that such species would receive a lower priority in recovery planning.

It also is unclear how priorities are to be balanced. It seems possible that all or most listed species might fall in one or more priority categories and could be a high priority in some regard, but allow priority in other. For example, the Florida panther might have a low priority for a recovery plan under the criteria, given its similarity to the other subspecies of *Felis concolor* and great difficulty in recovering, but it might have a high priority because it substantially conflicts with development.

Appointment of Recovery Team
    When a recovery plan is to be done, a recovery team would be appointed and requirements for the appointment process are set out as a new § 5(d) (pp. 106-107). Under current law, FACA would not apply. Team members would be "broadly representative of the constituencies with an interest in the species and its recovery and in the economic or social impacts of recovery..." Aside form this requirement, the balance of representation on a recovery team is left to the discretion of the Secretary. Members would also be selected for their knowledge of the species involved or expertise in the elements of the recovery plan or its implementation.

    A new § 5(d)(3) of the bill (p. 107) would authorize the Secretary to establish criteria to identify species for which the appointment of a recovery team would not be required. These criteria would have to take into account the availability of resources for recovery planning, the extent and complexity of the expected recovery activities, and the degree of scientific uncertainty associated with the threats to the species. There is no other clarification of what such criteria should be. If the Secretary does not appoint a recovery team, the Secretary may allow a state to complete a recovery plan. If a state does not do so, the Secretary must perform the duties of a recovery team.

Contents of Recovery Plans

Within 6 months of the formation of a recovery team, recommendations on recovery goals would be made to the Secretary by the members of the recovery team "with relevant scientific expertise." As mentioned, the recovery goals would be based *solely* on the best scientific and commercial data available. These recommendations would have to receive independent scientific review, which could prove difficult with respect to little-known species for which there are a limited number of experts. Under new § 5(e)(2) (p. 110), recovery plans would contain recovery measures designed to achieve the recovery goals. These recovery measures could include traditional measures such as actions to protect and restore habitat, but also the establishment of refuges, captive breeding, and releases of experimental populations. Under § 2(c)(8) of the bill (p. 97), any data that were described by the Secretary or submitted to the Secretary in connection with a listing regulation would be required to be considered by a recovery team and the Secretary.

In developing a draft recovery plan, a recovery team (or the Secretary if there is no recovery team) would be required to consider alternative measures to meet the recovery goals and "an appropriate balance" among enumerated factors of time, effectiveness, and social and economic impacts. No detail is provided on how the appropriateness of the balance of recovery measures would be determined, and absent additional guidance, a final decision of the Secretary on this matter might not be judicially reviewable.[10] A draft plan also would have to describe the economic effects of recommended recovery measures, describe alternative recovery measures that are not included with the reasons further inclusion or exclusion, and describe economic effects. A recovery plan also would have to include measurable benchmarks by which progress toward recovery could

---

[10] CHARLES H. KOCH, JR., ADMINISTRATIVE LAW AND PRACTICE § 13.3 92d ed.) (1977), discussing Citizens to Preserve Overton Park, Inc. v. Volpe, 401 U.S. 402 (1971) and other cases. Courts may be expressly precluded from reviewing agency actions, including instances when a subject is committed to agency discretion by law, or may be precluded from doing so in practice because of a lack of criteria or meaningful standards by which to evaluate agency decisions.

be measured. Specifying both recovery goals and measurable benchmarks could be difficult for species for which adequate information is not available.

Public Notice and Participation

Other provisions in new § 5(f) (p. 113) would provide for public notice and opportunity to comment, and for up to five hearings on a plan, including at least one in each state to which a plan would apply. Because this provision contains the same wording as does the new listing section and requires holding at lest one hearing "in an affected rural area, if any," ("rural area" is defined in § 9(a)(3) of the bill as a country or unincorporated area with no city or town over 10,000 inhabitants), it appears likely that the maximum of five hearings could be required in many instances. This process would probably broaden public participation, but could be costly and time-consuming.

Role of the Secretary

Under new § 5(h) (p. 114), the Secretary would review a draft recovery plan for compliance with the law and give the recovery team an opportunity to resubmit a plan to which the Secretary objected. In finalizing a plan, the Secretary would select recovery measures that meet the recovery goal and benchmarks and publish an explanation of why any measures recommended by the team were not selected. It is not clear whether the Secretary could modify the recovery goals and benchmarks or add additional recovery measures not recommended by the team. The selected measures must meet the balance required by § 5(e)(2)(B)(i) (concerning effectiveness, time, and social and economic impacts). Review of existing plans and periodic review and possible revision of new or existing plans would be permitted. Revisions would also be completed by recovery teams unless the Secretary has established an exception.

New § 5(d)(3) (p. 107) would authorize the Secretary to establish criteria for identifying species for which the appointment of a recovery team would not be required. If the Secretary does not appoint a recovery team, the Secretary shall allow a state to appoint a recovery team and complete a recovery plan. If a state does not appoint a recovery team, the Secretary must perform all the duties of a recovery team.

Implementation Agreements

Under new § 5(1)(1) (p. 116-117), the Secretary would be "authorized" to implement recovery measures by entering into agreements with federal agencies, states, Indian tribes, local governments, private landowners and organizations. (See previous comments concerning "tribes.") The bill sets out preliminary criteria for the Secretary's approval of such agreements, such as whether the party has the legal authority and capability to carry out the agreement. These agreements appear to be optional and there are no provisions regarding their contents. How these agreements interact with other implementation agreements authorized by the section (discussed below) is not clear.

In contrast to the apparently optional agreements authorized under new § 5(1)(1), under new § 5(1)(2) (p. 117), there would be a duty for each federal agency identified as an agency that authorizes, funds, or carries out actions likely to have significant effect on a listed species, to enter into an implementation agreement with the Secretary not later than 2 years after approval of a recovery plan.

"For purposes of satisfying this section" (*i.e.,* new ESA § 5), the substantive provisions of these agreements as "within the sole discretion of the Secretary and the head of the Federal agency entering into the agreement." This language would preclude judicial review of whatever is committed to the discretion of the officials negotiating such agreements.[11] However, the breadth of what is committed to their discretion is not clear. The committee report asserts that only review of a plan for compliance with § 5 would be precluded, and that review of compliance with the rest of the ESA and other laws would be retained.[12] Possibly this means that only the issue of whether the measures in a federal implementation agreement are adequate to achieve recovery is intended to be insulated from review. However, the language in question does place "the substantive provisions of the agreement" to some extent beyond review, and these provisions would include measures to be carried out on the lands. Arguably, this language leaves open the possibility of restrictive or permissive agreements or anything in between.

One could perhaps argue that even if federal recovery measures would be insulated from judicial review, judicial review would still be available for compliance of federal actions with the § 7(a) requirement that agencies avoid jeopardizing the continued existence of species. However, new § 5(1)(3) of the bill would provide that any action authorized in one of these agreements "shall not be subject to the requirements of section 7(a)(2) for that species," if the action is carried out during the term of the agreement and the agency is in compliance with the agreement. Section 7(a)(2) both requires that federal agencies insure that their

---

[11] *Id.*

[12] *See* S. Rep. 105-128 at 22 (1997), which states: "With the exception of the deadline for completion of recovery plan implementation agreements between the Secretary and a Federal agency, compliance of those agreements with section 5 would not be subject to judicial review under the provisions of section 11 of the Act. The agreement may be challenged as violative of other laws and other sections of the Act."

actions will not jeopardize the continued existence of listed species and requires completion of the consultation process to review federal actions for possible jeopardy. It is not clear whether new § 5(1)(3) would only eliminate the consultation process, or whether it also would eliminate the requirement of § 7(a)(2) that the agency insure that it will avoid jeopardy. (Other parts of the ESA, such as § 7(a)(1), provide a general duty to federal agencies to conserve species, but courts have focused on the more specific federal agencies to conserve species, but courts have focused on the more specific requirements and procedures of § 7(a)(2) in enforcement actions.) Therefore, the scope of the exceptions provided in new § 5(1) and the scope of remaining judicial review is not clear, and these issues go to the basic duties of federal agencies to ensure the survival and recovery of listed species.

No public involvement in the development of federal implementation agreements would be required. If the agency involved prepared an Environmental Impact Statement under the National Environmental Policy Act (NEPA), this process would appear to afford an opportunity for public participation, even though the final choices would be completely up to the Secretary and the head of the agency involved and be beyond judicial review. We do not know if similar instances exist where the EIS process is completed with public participation even though the final decision is within the unreviewable discretion of an official.

Furthermore, under new § 5(1)(3)(a) (P. 118), non-federal persons and their actions could be included in "an implementation agreement" if a site-specific action "meets the requirements of subparagraph (A)" and requires federal authorization or funding. Subparagraph (A0 refers to agreements between an agency and the Secretary. It is not clear which types of agreements non-federal parties can participate, but it appears that they may participate in both general agreements under new § 5(1)(1), which expressly mentions non-federal parties, and in mandatory agency agreements under § 5(1)(2). If private parties participate in mandatory federal agency agreements, it appears that the actions of private parties could also be excused from the consultation process, and not be subject to public input or judicial review.[13]

As noted under new § 5(1)(3)(A) (p. 118), agency actions that affect listed species or critical habitat apparently would not be subject to § 7 consultation if the action is addressed in an implementation agreement and the federal agency is in compliance with the agreement. Therefore, only agency scientists would review agency actions or non-federal actions included in such an agreement. Federal agency efforts to recover species would be almost completely up to the individual

---

[13] This interpretation appears to be supported by the committee report at 23.

agency, checked only by the requirement that the Secretary must initially agree to the implementation plan. This arguably may increase efficiency and agencies could be expected to make good faith efforts to carry out the law. However, agencies have not always made adequate efforts in the past.[14] The bill lacks the usual checks on agency actions, such as meaningful public input, non-agency review, peer review, and judicial review. The adequacy (or inadequacy) of an agency's decisions may not become clear until species in question have declined further. And, as noted, non-federal actions could also be included in these agency implementation agreements.

The relationship of these provisions on recovery to existing processes of federal land management agencies is not clear. For example, a representative of a federal agency affected by a particular recovery effort *may* be a recovery team, but representation of such agencies would not be required. Recovery plan implementation of such agencies would not be required. Recovery plan implementation agreements with federal agencies would be required, but the relationship of these agreements to existing federal land management plans is not specified. Perhaps in the context of federal land management agencies, the implementation agreements would be the specific measures and timetables proposed by an agency to respond to a recovery plan through making plan amendments or revisions. If so, because such plan amendments would occur after an agency implementation agreement, which could be executed up to 2 year after approval of a recovery plan, the time for federal agency response could be very long. As drafted, there is no provision for emergency responses.

Financial assistance to private landowners in carrying out a recovery plan implementation agreement would be made available under the provisions of new § 5(1)(4).

FACA
As under current law, FACA would not apply to recovery teams.

Role of States
The Secretary would be required under new § (a) to "develop and implement" recovery plans "in cooperation with the States." Section 9(a)(2) of the bill would add a new paragraph to § 3 of the ESA defining "in cooperation with the States,"

---

[14] For example, one judge commented that the Forest Service in its actions to conserve the northern spotted owl had engaged in "a remarkable series of violations of the environmental laws...;" had exhibited a "deliberate and systematic refusal" to comply with the laws; and that "[t]he problem here has not been any shortcoming in the laws, but simply a refusal of administrative agencies to comply with them." Seattle Audubon Society v. Evans, 771 F. Supp. 1081, 1089, 1090, 1096 (W.D. Wash. 1991).

as a process under which each of the affected states or a representative of state agencies would be given an opportunity to "participate in a meaningful and timely manner in the development of the standards, guidelines, and regulations to implement [the act]." There is no elaboration on how state representatives would participate or who would develop the "process" by which that participation takes place, though it may be inferred that the Secretary would do so. While this provision would allow states to represent their interests in species and recovery plans, it also raises questions as to how this participation in both the development and implementation of plans is to occur and how state participation might affect the statutory deadlines.

In addition, under new § 5(m) (p. 120), upon the request of one or more Governors, the Secretary may authorize a state agency to prepare a recovery plan in accordance with the scheduling, team appointment, and general substantive requirements of the federal law. The Secretary "in cooperation with the States" would publish standards and guidelines for the development of recovery plans "and for the grant and withdrawal of authorization by the Secretary..." It is not clear whether "with the States" here refers only to a particular instance in which a recovery plan would be developed by a state or states. Or whether these standards and guidelines would be general ones developed to guide all instances when states would develop recovery plans. Additional provisions regarding when the Secretary may withdraw authority form a state are set out. The Secretary must give the state agency an opportunity to correct deficiencies identified by the Secretary and unless the deficiencies are cured within 60 days, the Secretary may withdraw authority from the state. (Interestingly, if the deficiency is a missed deadline for developing a draft recovery plan, this appears to extend the delay by 60 or more days.)

New § 5 (d)(3) (p. 107) would authorize the Secretary to establish criteria for identifying species for which the appointment of a recovery team would not be required. If the Secretary does not appoint a recovery team, the Secretary shall allow a state to appoint a recovery team and complete a recovery plan. If a state does not appoint a recovery team, the Secretary must perform all the duties of a recovery team.

Critical Habitat
    The new provisions in S. 1180 on the designation of critical habitat are in new ESA § 5(n) (p.123), which would require a recovery team to provide the Secretary with recommendations on critical habitat. Therefore, designation of critical habitat could occur a significant length of time after listing. (See *Habitat Protection* below.) This subsection is not among the subsections with which state-developed

recovery plans must comply. See § 5(m)(1), which requires a state plan to comply with various procedural sections and also with the substantive requirements of § 5(e). Therefore, the actions that would be required from state recovery teams with respect to critical habitat are not clear. Also, general guidance t landowners may not be available for quite some time after listing since designation of critical habitat, establishment of recovery measures, and management restriction could be set out in the recovery plan. In addition, § 2(c)(7)(C) would strike the language in current ESA § 4(b)(8) that requires the Secretary, as part of a designation of critical habitat accompanying a listing, to indicate which activities might adversely modify habitat.

Schedule/Deadlines

Under new § 5(c) (p. 106), a draft recovery plan would have to be completed not later than 18 months after listing and a final recovery plan finalized not later than 30 months after listing. An additional 2 years would be allowed for a federal agency recovery implementation agreement; plus additional time—which could easily be two years—would be needed to amend or revise federal land and resource management plans thereafter. Therefore, for a species that occurs on federal lands, 61/2 years could elapse between the time a species is listed and the time protective measures were in place under relevant federal management plans. Listing itself and possible litigation would additional time. No provision is made for emergency responses.

Reports

The Secretary would be required to report every 2 years to the relevant congressional committees on the status of efforts to develop recovery plans.

Enforcement

Section 3 (c) of the bill (p. 128) would amend § 11 (g)(1)(C) of the Act to allow citizen suits against *the Secretary* for failing to perform any act or duty under new § 5 on recovery plans which is not discretionary with the Secretary. The principal remedy in the context of a state-developed recovery plan appears to be for the Secretary to remove the authority provided the state. A citizen suit might be available to force the Secretary to take that action in some circumstances. As discussed above, judicial review of recovery implementation agreements negotiated with a federal agency would be circumscribed and the extent of review is unclear. These agreements also apparently could include actions by non-federal parties that receive federal approval or funding. (See *Enforcement* below.)

H.R. 2351

Section 2 (8) finds that only by taking actions that implement "the existing recovery goal" of the ESA "Can we ensure that species will eventually be removed from the lists" under the Act.

Duty to Recover Species
Section 107(a) of the bill (pp. 16-17) would amend § 7(a) of the ESA to clarify that the current requirement that all federal agencies use their authorities to further the purposes of the ESA by carrying out programs for the conservation of listed species includes recovery actions identified in recovery implementation plans of the agency. Some duty to recover species appears to be currently required because of the definition of the word "conserve" in § 3 of the ESA, but the House bill would clarify this duty.

As is true of S. 1180, H.R. 2351 would significantly broaden existing ESA recovery provisions and add new provisions. Section 2(8) of the bill (p.4) would find that implementing the recovery goal of the ES is necessary to ensure that species will eventually be removed from the ESA lists. Section 101 (p. 5) would define "recovery" to mean "that the threats to a species, as analyzed under section 4(a), have been eliminated, the species has achieved long-term viability, and the protective measures under this Act are no longer needed." As will be discussed, this reference to the elimination of threats could have broad effects.

When Recovery Plan Required
Section 105 (p. 12) would amend current ESA § 4(f) that addresses recovery plans. In contrast to the Senate bill, H.R. 2351 would require a recovery plan to be prepared for "each" endangered or threatened species and would strike the current exception that allows the Secretary not to prepare a recovery plan if the Secretary finds that a plan will not promote the conservation of the species. On the one hand, this requirement could encourage preparation of multi-species recovery plans, but on the other hand, it could be a very difficult requirement to meet without more personnel and funds. Arguably, it could also waste time and money on recovery plans that would not promote the conservation of species.

Contents of Recovery Plans
Section 105 (p. 13) would add new language to require that recovery plans include provisions for the conservation in the recovery plan area of each species listed as endangered species or threatened species, and for "candidate species, and species proposed for listing." It is not clear how or why "recovery" provisions

should be prepared for species that are not yet listed, since before listing it has not been determined that the protective measures of listing are necessary and hence that recovery can be achieved. The intention might be to require that a recovery plan include provisions relative to candidate and proposed species in the area that "would be likely to eliminate the need for listing," but this is not stated.

The provisions of current § 4(f)(1)(C) that describe the contents of recovery plans would be modified (p. 13) to require that the description of site-specific management actions denote those of the "highest priority and greatest recovery potential." Habitat needs the population levels would be included among the objective measurable criteria that, when met, would be included among the objective measurable criteria that, when met, would result in a determination that a species could be removed from listing. (p. 14). Current law requiring estimates of time and costs would not be changed. A new provision added as § 4(f)(1)(C)(iv) (p. 14) would require a general description of types of actions likely to violate the taking and jeopardy prohibitions. This would provide additional guidance to landowners. Unlike S. 1180, the bill would retain current § 4(b)(8), that requires the Secretary to publish, at the time of critical habitat designation, information on activities that would adversely affect the habitat.

Another new provision (p. 14) would require a list of federal, state, tribal, and local government entities that would be significantly affected by the goals or management actions in the recovery plan, and should complete a recovery implementation plan under new ESA § 4(f)(5)(A). However, new § 4(f)(5)(A) (p. 15) would only require federal agencies to develop plans, so the duties of non-federal agencies in this regard are unclear.

Federal Implementation Plans
New ESA § 4(f)(5)(A) (pp. 15-16) would require each federal agency significantly affected by the goals or management actions in a final recovery plan to develop and implement a recovery implementation plan after public notice and opportunity for comment. Such a plan would have to identify the agency's duties and management responsibilities that would contribute to the achievement of the recovery goals' set forth specific agency actions, timetables, and funding to achieve and monitor recovery goals, identify lands or waters under the agency's jurisdiction that do or could provide habitat of the species; identify any actions needed to acquire additional suitable habitat; and describe those actions the agency will take to contribute to recovery. Presumably, the timetables would reflect any time necessary to amend or revise land and resource management plans where appropriate. It appears that failure by an agency to carry out a

recovery implementation plan could be challenged under the citizen suit provisions of §11(g)(1) of the ESA as amended by § 109 of the bill (p. 43).

Schedule/Deadlines

Section 105 (p. 12) would amend ESA §4(f) to require completion of a draft recovery plan within 18 months and a final plan within 30 months. Implementation is also stated as beginning after 30 months (p. 13), but under new § 4(f)(5)(A), agencies are to develop a "recovery implementation plan" after a recovery plan is finalized and after notice and opportunity for public review and comment. No specific length of time is set out for completion of these agreements. Additional time would be consumed by any necessary amendments or revisions to federal land and resource management plans. There are no provisions for emergency responses. Therefore, the House and Senate bills would probably involve similar length of time for federal agencies to respond with recovery actions.

Role of States

New § 4(f)(5)(C) (p.16) would direct the Secretary, consistent with current ESA § 6 on cooperative agreements, to cooperate to the maximum extent practicable with states, tribes, and local government entities that are significantly affected by a final recovery plan, to develop cooperative plans to achieve the goals of a recovery plan. ESA § 6 would be amended (p.16) to include "any Indian tribe" as a possible party with whom the Secretary could enter into a cooperative agreement. (See earlier discussion concerning recognized and unrecognized tribes.)

Determining Recovery

Under new § 4(f)(1)(D) (p.14), for the purpose of determining criteria for measuring when a species has recovered and can be de-listed, the Secretary, in consultation with the National Academy of Sciences, would be required to select a panel of scientists with related expertise and no significant economic interest in the recovery plan. How the Secretary is to work with the panel is not set out, but it appears that the panel is to determine the criteria and the Secretary is to apply to make de-listing determinations.

HABITAT PRESERVATION

Current Law

Under current law, habitat is protected in several ways. It is protected directly through designation of critical habitat and acquisition of habitat; and indirectly through issuance of incidental take permits, cooperative agreements with states, and the inclusion of significant habitat destruction within the take prohibitions through the definition of "harm" contained in current regulations.[15]

The ESA provides for the designation of critical habitat at the time of listing. This designation may affect what actions are allowed and how actions are structured, modified, or mitigated as a result of § 7 consultations involving federal actions or non-federal actions with a federal nexus. Designated critical habitat may also factor into an evaluation of "harm" under the take prohibitions of § 9, by possibly making it easier to demonstrate the extent of injury and disruption required under the implementing regulations.

Under § 4(a)(3) of the ESA, "to the maximum extend prudent and determinable," the Secretary shall designate critical habitat for species being listed as endangered or threatened at the time of listing.[16] Under § 4(b), the Secretary is to designate habitat after considering and weighing various factors:

> The Secretary shall designate critical habitat, and make revisions thereto under subsection (a)(3) on the basis of the best scientific data available and after taking into consideration the economic impact, and any other relevant impact, of specifying any particular area as critical habitat. The Secretary may exclude any area from critical habitat if he determines that the benefits of such exclusion outweigh the benefits of specifying such area as part of the critical habitat, unless he determines, base on the best scientific and commercial data available, that the failure to designate such area as critical habitat will result in the extinction of the species concerned.

Under current § 4(b)(8), whenever the Secretary publishes a listing regulation that includes or revises critical habitat, the summary accompanying the regulation shall, "to the maximum extent practicable, also include a brief description and

---

[15] 50 C.F.R. § 17.3 defines harm as: "an act which actually kills or injures wildlife. Such act may include significant habitat modification or degradation where it actually kiss or injures wildlife by significantly impairing essential behavioral patterns, including breeding, feeding or sheltering." This regulation was sustained by the Supreme Court in Babbitt v. Sweet Home Chapter of Communities for Great Oregon, 515 U.S. 687 (1995).

[16] In practice, designation at the time of listings is extremely unusual, possibly due to costs or low agency priority. In fact, as of May 31, 1997, only 124 species had designated critical habitat.

evaluation of those activities (whether public or private) which, in the opinion of the Secretary, if undertaken may adversely modify such habitat, or may be affected by such designation." This provides some guidance to landowners as to when they might need to obtain a permit under § 10 for harmful activities.

Section 10 authorizes various exceptions to the § p prohibitions that otherwise would apply. Habitat may be protected through the issuance of "incidental take" permits to non-federal persons under § 10(a) of the Act. This allows otherwise prohibited takes of listed species if the takes are incidental to otherwise lawful activities and the applicant submits a conservation plan that meets the requirements of that subsection (usually referred to as a "habitat conservation plan" or HCP). To approve a conservation plan and issue a § 10 permit, the Secretary must find that: the taking will be incidental; the applicant will, to the maximum extent practicable, minimize and mitigate the impacts of such taking; the applicant will ensure that adequate funding for the plan will be provided; the taking will not appreciably reduce the likelihood of the survival and recovery of the species in the wild; and any additional measures required by the Secretary will be met. The Secretary must also have received whatever other assurances the Secretary requires that the plan will be implemented.

Although the § 10(a) permit process was little used in the past, many more permits have been issued recently. Several policies were put in place administratively that facilitate the § 10 process. "Safe Harbor" allows a landowner to improve habitat and later return to the previous level without penalty. "No Surprises," allows the Secretary to negotiate agreements to which (basically) new requirements cannot be added without the landowner's consent, although the government in some circumstances can intervene at its own expense.[17] Other measures provide small landowner exemptions and streamlined processes. Proponents assert that these measures help to remedy the current disincentives that can discourage owners from maintaining or restoring habitat. Opponents question whether the measures are authorized by current law and whether they adequately protect listed species. The "no surprises" policy, in particular, has been questioned because of the difficulty in crafting conservation agreements, e.g. how to balance the desirability of long-term agreements that would provide more accurate estimates of the amount of quality of habitat over a meaningful length of time versus the desirability of having the agreements be short enough to adjust for changed circumstances. Some ecological conditions require a long time to be

---

[17] The Fish and Wildlife Service and the National Oceanic and Atmospheric Administration jointly proposed a "No surprises" rule in response to the March 21, 1997 settlement agreement in Spirit of the Sage v. Babbitt, No. 1:96CV02503 (§)(D.D.C.), 62 FED. REG. 29091 (May 29, 1997). A final rule has not been published at 63 FED. REG. 8859 (February 23, 1998).

produced (*e.g.* late-successional forests), which might argue for a long-term agreement, yet future conditions can be difficult to envision and provide for adequately (*e.g.* the rapidity with which personal motor vehicles, highways, and suburban sprawl has occurred).

Habitat may be acquired by the government under current § 5. Habitat may also be conserved under cooperative agreements with one or more states under § 6. Lastly, some protection of habitat against significant destruction is encompassed with the current regulatory definition of "harm" as part of the takings of listed species that are prohibited under § 9.

Both bills would build on current law. Both would include at least some versions of the recent administrative changes as new law, and both attempt to build in incentives for private landowners to cooperate in providing habitats for listed species.

See also, *Incentives for Private Landowners.*

S. 1180

The Senate bill would affect habitat conservation in several ways. The current provisions on land acquisition would be retained as new § 5A, and § 6 on cooperative agreements with states would also be retained.

Designation of Critical Habitat

Section 2(c)(2) of the bill (p. 87) would amend § 4 of the ESA to eliminate the current requirement that the Secretary designate critical habitat concurrently with the listing of a species. Under § 3(b) of the bill (p. 123), new ESA § 5(n) would contain the provisions on designation of critical habitat, which would now be done in connection with recovery planning. A recovery team, if one is appointed, would make recommendations for critical habitat and special habitat management considerations to the Secretary. These recommendations would be due within 9 months of a final listing regulation. Then, under new ESA § 5(n)(2) (p. 124), not later than 18 months after the date on which a final listing is made, the Secretary, after consultation and in cooperation with the recovery team, would publish a proposed regulation designating critical habitat for a species, with a final regulation to follow within 30 months after listing. Recovery plans are to be developed in cooperation with affected states as well. As a general matte, therefore, designation of critical habitat would be required within 30 months of listing in instances when a recovery plan is prepared. If a recovery plan is not developed, the Secretary would be required to publish a final critical habitat determination for a listed species not later than 3 years after listing (p. 125). The Secretary may designate critical habitat concurrently with a final listing regulation if the Secretary determines that designation at that time is essential to avoid the imminent extinction of the species.

It is not clear what happens with respect to designation of critical habitat when a state prepares a recovery plan. In developing plans, states would be required to comply with the substantive requirements of recovery plans contained in new ESA § 5(e) (pp. 109-113), but the critical habitat designation provisions would be in new § 5(n) (p. 124), so the extent to which a state would be required to address critical habitat is not clear. It appears that state recovery team planners would make recommendations to the Secretary, who then would make the designation.

The factors the Secretary would consider when designating critical habitat under the new provisions would be similar to those in current law, except that the additional factor of "impacts to military training and operations" would be required to be considered. The current language on excluding habitat would be preserved.

A new process for petitioning for revision of critical habitat would be provided in new ESA § 5(n)(6) (pp. 126-127). This process would parallel the current process for petitions to list—requiring a finding of whether the petition presents substantial scientific or commercial information indicating that revision may be warranted. Upon making this finding, the Secretary would publish a notice of how the Secretary intends to proceed. A regulation to designate or revise critical habitat would proceed in the same manner as a listing regulation.

Guidance to Landowners

Section 2(c)(7)(C) of the bill (p. 96) would strike the current provisions that requires guidance for landowners as to what activities might adversely modify habitat of listed species. Perhaps the new provision for a recovery team to recommend areas of critical habitat "and any recommendations for special management considerations or protection that are specific to the habitat" is meant to replace the current landowner-guidance provision. However, there is no requirement for the Secretary to act on recovery plan recommendations, or to include special management considerations and protections in a final designation of critical habitat.

Section 9(c) of the bill (pp. 173-174) would add another type of agreement to § 9 of the ESA to authorize a non-federal property owner to enter in an agreement to identify activities of the property owner that will not result in a violation of the taking prohibitions of § 9. However, the Secretary, the Attorney General, or any other person could still begin an enforcement action under § 11. Therefore, these "agreements" are more akin to advisory opinions, although in practice they might carry some weight. These agreements appear to replace the current § 11. Therefore, these "agreements" are more akin to advisory opinions, although in practice they might carry some weight. These agreements appear to replace the current § 4(b)(8) description of activities that might adversely modify habitat. Note that the current descriptions of activities are necessarily general; whether the Secretary would be able to respond adequately to *individual* landowners under the new provisions, and do so within the required 90-day period appears doubtful. In addition, landowners might seek these agreements in lieu of submitting conservation plans.

State Agreements on Proposed or Candidate Species

Section 2(c)(12) of the bill (pp. 101-102) would amend § 4 of the ESA to add new express authority for the Secretary to enter into agreements with one or more states for the conservation not only of listed species into agreements with one or more states for the conservation not only of listed species (as is permitted now), but also of species that are proposed for listing or are likely to become a candidate species I the near future. Such agreements might address necessary habitat, but this is not expressly stated.

Federal Implementation Plans

As discussed in Recovery Plans above, under new ESA § 5(1)(2) (p. 117), federal agencies and the Secretary would enter into mandatory recovery implementation agreements, the contents of which, for purposes of the recovery section, would be totally within the discretion of the agency and the Secretary and hence insulated from judicial review. The requirements of current § 7(a)(2) on consultation and avoiding jeopardy also appear not to apply to these agreements and the agreements can include actions by non-federal parties if those actions receive federal approval or funding. Therefore, it is possible that some actions that do not comply with current law might be included in these agreements and be insulated from review. The effects of such agreements on habitat are therefore difficult to assess.

General § 10 Provisions

Section 5 of the bill would expand the current § 10 provisions on conservation plans to provide various opportunities for property owners to undertake measures to conserve species. The current provisions of § 10 with respect to listed species would be preserved, and under § 10 permits to take species on the high seas as well as within the United States and its territorial waters as is the case under current law. In addition, under § 9(5) of the bill (p. 173), "territorial sea" would be defined to mean the 12-nautical mile maritime zone set out in Presidential Proclamation No. 5928, dated December 27, 1988, rather than its current meaning of (generally) three miles.[18] Given the widely accepted legal meaning of this term, use of a different term such as "maritime zone" in this context might avoid confusion. The new definition would allow the Secretary to issue incidental take permits for species such as salmon, various whales, birds, and sea turtles in waters for which § 10 permits have not been issued and therefore this language represents a broadening of current applicability.

Monitoring
Under §5(b) of the bill (p. 143) the Secretary would expressly be authorized to require submission of monitoring data. There is no general duty for the Secretary to monitor conservation plans.

Multiple Species Plans
Section 5(c) of the bill (p. 143) addresses multiple species conservation plans. As discussed above, current law authorizes the Secretary to issue an incidental take permit if the Secretary approves a conservation plan that meets the requirements of the Act. New provisions in S. 1180 would provide that a conservation plan covering listed species could also include—at the request of the applicant—proposed, candidate, or "other species" if the Secretary were satisfied that the permit application met the requirements for listed species and the new requirements with respect to any other species. If any of the species covered by the agreement then is listed, a permit would automatically take effect for parties in compliance with an agreement, presumably on the same terms as the agreement.

The first of the new requirements (p. 144) for a multiple species permit would be that the impacts of the plan on "non-listed" species would be "incidental." The term incidental is also used in current § 10(a)(2)(B), where it apparently refers to its use as part of the phrase "incidental to otherwise lawful activity." If that is the sense in which the term is intended in the new requirement, use of the entire phrase could avoid the possibility of the term being interpreted as having its other meaning "of minor consequence."

The next new requirement would be for the applicant, to the maximum extent practicable, to minimize and mitigate impacts. The necessity for this requirement

---

[18] *See,* United States v. California, 332 U.S. 19, 33-34 (1947) and sources cited there.

could be questioned to the extent it would apply to "other" species that are neither listed, proposed, nor candidate species, and which may in fact be plentiful.

The Secretary would also be required to find under new § 10(a)(3)(B)(ii)(p. 144), that the actions of the applicant with respect to proposed or candidate species, "if undertaken by all similarly situated persons within the range of species, would be likely to eliminate the need to list the species as an endangered species or a threatened species for the duration of the agreement..." This provision appears intended to improve the status of the species in question and to distribute the burden of providing assistance to the species in question among all the landowners available in an area. On the one hand, this would ensure that no one owner could carry a disproportionate share of the beneficial actions that are needed. On the other hand, absent some assurance that other landowners would also participate, it is not clear whether this approach would afford sufficient protection overall, since the penalties of the Act would not apply to takes of proposed or candidate species until they are listed. Under new § 10(a)(3)(F) (pp. 146-147), a § 10 permit would be issued for species included in a multiple-species agreement once those species are listed. Therefore, actions allowed under a before-listing agreement that were premised on other actions hypothetically being taken that might not materialize, would apparently continue to be allowed once the species is listed. Continuation of such actions might become harmful once a species had dropped to the point of needing the protection of the ESA. Perhaps if the benefit of this lesser burden was extended only to those owners participating in area-wide agreements this might encourage more owners to join in broader, area-wide efforts in order to achieve the least burdensome restrictions for their individual properties. Arguably, such area-wide agreements could provide a more sound basis for post-listing protections, since the commitments by landowners would be actual rather than hypothetical.

Also, depending on the duration of an agreement, these agreements cold provide an opportunity to halt the decline of proposed or candidate species, or could result in a drop in numbers of the proposed or candidate species after the end of the term of the agreement.[19] As drafted, there is no requirement that the Secretary take into account the relationship of the duration of the agreement to the likelihood of eliminating the need to list the species, given the actions an applicant seeks to carry out and the conditions likely to exist by the end of the agreement.

---

[19] For example, if the term of an agreement was short relative to the lifespan of the species involved, existing individuals could live to the end of the agreement term, but there could be a significant drop in numbers of individuals thereafter if habitat was not maintained so as to produce new generations.

With respect to agreements involving non-listed species other than proposed or candidate species, new language (pp. 144-145) would be added as § 10 (a)(3)(B)(Iv) requiring the Secretary to find that actions taken by the applicant, if undertaken by all similarly situated persons within the range of the other non-listed species, would not be likely to contribute to a determination to list such species for the duration of the agreement. This is similar to the provision discussed above and similar comments can be offered. However, because the species involved may not be in decline, the required level of response under this provision would be merely to avoid contributing to a determination to list the species.

Technical assistance would be made available in new § 10(a)(3)(C) (p. 145) for the development of multi-species agreements and these agreements would be subject to public notice and comment.

Section 5(e) of the bill (p. 153) would amend § 10(c) of the ESA to provide for, with the approval of the applicant, public participation in the *development* of a multiple species conservation plan and permit application. This contrasts with p. 143 of the bill that states that the Secretary could approve a qualifying multiple-species conservation plan and issue a permit after notice and opportunity for public comment. Another part of § 5(e) states that if a multiple species conservation plan is developed without an opportunity for public participation, the Secretary should extend the public comment period for an additional 30 days.

Note that the multiple species agreements duplicate the concepts and terms of the agreements for candidate species (which also include proposed species and other species) discussed below.

Low-Effect Permits

A streamlined process for permits for low-effect activities would be added as new ESA § 10(a)(4) (pp. 147-148). These permits would provide a faster, less expensive process for applicants whose proposed activities would not be likely to have significant impacts. A low-effect permit could be issued if the Secretary determines that the activity will have no more than a "negligible effect, both individually and cumulatively" on the species, "any taking associated with the activity will be incidental, and the taking will not appreciably reduce the likelihood of the survival and recovery of the species in the wild." These permits would require appropriate actions to be taken by the permittee to offset the effect of the permitted activity on the species. Again, it is not clear, especially in the context, whether the term "incidental" is intended to mean "incidental to otherwise lawful activity" or "of minor consequence." The Secretary is directed to develop "model permit applications that will constitute conservation plans for low effect activities." Given the diversity of activities that may qualify for low-effects permits, an alternate approach might simply authorize the Secretary to develop streamlined processes for low-effect activities.

"No Surprises" Provisions
A new § 10(a)(5) (pp. 148-149) would enact the "no surprises" concept by requiring each conservation plan developed under subsection (a) of § 10 to have a no surprises provision. (Possibly this language should refer to permits rather than plans here.) The no surprises language would provide that a person who has entered into and is in compliance with a conservation plan may not be required to undertake additional mitigation measures for species covered by the pan that would require additional money or the adoption of additional use restrictions on otherwise available land, waters, or "water-related rights" without the consent of the permittee. It is not clear what effect the inclusion of the phrase "water-related rights" would have, and this point is not clarified in the committee report.[20] It is possible, for example, that water received under contract from Bureau of Reclamation facilities, which apparently currently can be reduced in times of drought or for ESA-compliance purposes and other reasons under a standard term in such contracts, might not be able to be so reduced.[21]

The language also states (p. 149) that the Secretary and the applicant, *by the terms of the conservation plan,* may identify modifications to the plan or other additional measures that the Secretary may require under extraordinary circumstances, but not at the expense of the permittee. The statutory language does not state that these are the only modifications allowed. It is not clear exactly how the agreements are to anticipate the unforeseen. It appears that these agreed-upon terms could constitute advance consent by a permittee to additional requirements that could be imposed on the permitee under the circumstances articulated in the agreement. It is not clear to what extend the Secretary could impose additional requirements, aid from the terms of an agreement, under which the federal government could implement additional measures at the expense of the government. For example, there is no curtailment of the basic eminent domain authority of the government, under which the Secretary might, for example, condemn as easement in order to accomplish additional protections upon payment of compensation to the landowner.

The possibility that the Secretary could impose additional requirements, as long as the property owner does not pay, is supported by the language creating the

---

[20] S. Rep. 105-128 at 33 (1997).
[21] *See* O'Neill v. United States, 50 F. 3d 677, (9th Cir. 1995).

Habitat Conservation Insurance Program in § 5(m) of the bill (p. 161). This Program is to finance additional measures "not anticipated and addressed" in § 10(a) plans. Payments may be made to "any party" to a conservation plan under § 10(a). This apparently may apply to the government. The report language does not reconcile the language on the Program that refers to additional unanticipated measures with the "no surprises" provisions that refer to agreed upon modifications in extraordinary circumstances. The report states that the negotiated changes are the "only" modifications allowed.[22]

Other issues related to reopening the agreements could arise; if the correct interpretation is that the Secretary could carry out additional conservation measures, but at the expense of the government, how the Secretary would do so, considering private lands are involved is not specifically addressed. Also, it is not clear how much agencies could do to carry out the new responsibilities, given the chronic inability of personnel to complete current responsibilities.

The issue of what changes the Secretary might be able to make under the no surprises provisions is also relevant to how much flexibility the federal government might retain with respect to the management of its own lands—if the federal government cannot accomplish additional protective measures on private lands, even at its own expense, would the federal government be obligated to rely on federal lands more heavily to provide additional conservation measures in case of unplanned impacts and natural disasters?

Revocation

Under § 5(c) of the bill (p. 149), a new paragraph (6) would be added to § 19(a) of the ESA to authorize the Secretary to revoke any permits for excused takes *issued under subsection (a)* after notice and an opportunity for correction. It is not clear whether a permittee could be charged with § 9 takings during the time allowed for correction of noncompliance, or whether a permittee could only be charged after permit revocation. The revocation provision would apply to all the types of agreements issued under § 10(a) of the Act, but would not appear to apply to similar agreements place outside § 19(a) such as the safe harbor agreements and possibly the candidate species agreements. Candidate species agreements would be a new subsection (k) to § 10, which placement would seem to indicate the revocation provisions would not apply to them. However,

---

[22] S. Rep. 105-128 states at 34: "The bill recognizes that under certain circumstances, conditions may change in such a way as to warrant some modification to the conservation measures under an approved HCP. The Secretary, *under the terms of the plan as negotiated by the parties,* may *only* modify the conservation program of an HCP under extraordinary circumstances, but in no instance

candidate permits would be cross-referenced in § 10(a)(1), so possibly the revocation provisions wee meant to apply. If the revocation provisions would not apply, it is uncertain what recourse and remedies might be available to the Secretary for non-compliance with the terms of candidate agreements.

Candidate Species Agreements

Section 5(d) of the bill (p. 149) would add a new subsection (k) to § 10 of the ESA to provide separately for conservation agreements involving species that are proposed, candidate, or "likely to become a candidate species in the near future on property owned or under the jurisdiction of the person requesting such an agreement." Most of the provisions on these agreements would not be a part of current § 10(a) where many other new provisions on conservation plans would be place, including the multiple species agreements that are so similar. Yet, as discussed above, permits issued based on a candidate species agreement once a species is listed, *are* included in subsection (a). Agreements under this part differ from the new multi-species plans in that they do not involve listed species and they refer to species likely to become candidate species rather than "other species." Since interpretive issues may arise, Congress may decide to consolidate these types of agreements or to provide other clarification. Likewise, since safe harbor agreements and habitat reserve agreements are place outside § 10(a), it might be helpful to specify which general provisions (such as those on revocation, public participation, no surprises, and rulemaking) apply to which types of agreements under that § 10.

"Safe Harbor" Agreements

Section 5(f) of the bill (p. 153) would add new subsection (1) to § 10 of the ESA to authorize "safe harbor" agreements. These agreements are similar to the current administrative initiative of the same name. The new statutory language would provide that if a person creates, restores, maintains, or improves habitat, the Secretary shall permit the person to take listed species included in the agreement, incidental to other lawful activities, down to a baseline level that was agreed to in advance. This baseline may be expressed in terms of the abundance or distribution of listed species, quantity or quality of habitat, or other appropriate indicators. The Secretary is to issue standards and guidelines for the development and approval of safe harbor agreements. The bill (p. 155) also would make financial assistance available to landowners in carrying out these agreements. The assistance would be in addition to assistance available under other federal programs, but actions that

---

may the modification require the payment of additional money or the adoption of additional use,

are otherwise required under a permit, the ESA, or other laws, would not be eligible.

Safe harbor agreements are intended to encourage landowners to provide additional habitat and seem likely to contribute to that result. It is uncertain, however, (whether these agreements are statutory or not) whether it will prove possible to adequately determine baselines and enforce these agreements. Because the safe harbor agreements would be located outside § 10(a), it appears advisable to clarify that the Secretary may permit takes of listed species *that would otherwise be prohibited under* § 9 of the ESA. This language is used in current § 19(a) to make clear that authorized takes are excused under the ESA, and the same language could be used for other, non- § 10(a) permits.

Habitat Reserve Agreements

Section 5(g) of the bill (pp. 156-158) would add a new subsection (m) to § 10 to authorize habitat reserve agreements. These agreements would be implemented through contracts or easements to assist non-federal property owners in preserving and managing suitable habitat for listed species. The Secretary would be required to pay owners for carrying out these agreements unless the activities in question are otherwise required by the ESA. The Secretary would issue standards and guidelines for the development and approval of these agreements. The agreements would include provisions on duration and on specific management measures the owner would implement, the conditions under which the property could be used, and the nature and schedule for payments. It is not clear whether these agreements may authorize "takes" of listed species.

Financial Assistance

The bill would authorize $40,833,33 for payments for habitat reserve agreements. (These funds would have to be appropriated.) Section 5(h) (pp. 158-159) would provide additional financial assistance to states and political subdivisions of a state in developing conservation plans under a new Habitat Conservation Planning Loan Program. Section 5(m) of the bill (p. 161), would add a new subsection (n) to § 10 of the ESA to establish a Habitat Conservation Insurance Program that would be available to pay the cost of additional mitigation measures under a § 19(a) conservation plan or a candidate conservation agreement to minimize or mitigate adverse effects that were not anticipated and addressed at the time the agreement was approved. These grants are to be made to any person who is a party to a conservation plan or candidate conservation agreement.

---

development or management restrictions without the consent of the permittee." (Emphasis added.)

Therefore, it appears that these funds may be used to compensate owners who agree to additional measures.

Miscellaneous

Section 5(i) of the bill (p. 160) states that nothing in the section requires modification of existing permits and plans. Section 5(j) (P. 160) would require that final rules implementing the amended § 10 (a) be completed by not later than a year of enactment after notice and opportunity for public comment.

Section 5(1) of the bill would add details on how the Secretary may issue § 10 permits for scientific purposes. Section 5(m) (pp. 161-162) would add a new subsection (m) to § 10 to create a Habitat Conservation Insurance Program to finance additional mitigation measures that were not anticipated in § 10(a) plans or candidate conservation agreements.

Other educational opportunities and technical assistance would be provided under § 7 of the bill.

Report

Section 5(k) (p. 160) would require the Secretaries, not later than two years after enactment, to enter into "appropriate arrangements" with the National Academy of Sciences to prepare a report on the development and implementation of conservation plans under § 10(a) of the ESA. Some of the types of conservation agreements are not under § 10(a). The report would assess the extent to which plans comply with the requirements of the ESA, the role of multiple species conservation plans in preventing the need to list species covered by those plans, and the relationship of conservation plans for listed species to implementation of recovery plans. This report would be sent to Congress not later than 5 years after enactment.

Advisory "Agreements"

Section 9(c) of the bill (pp. 173-174) would add another type of "agreement" to § 9 of the ESA to authorize a non-federal property owner to enter into an agreement in identifying activities of the property owner that would not result in a violation of the taking of prohibitions of § 9. However, the Secretary, the Attorney General, or any other person could still being an enforcement action under § 11. Therefore, these "agreements" might be characterized a advisory opinions, although what weight a court might give them is uncertain. These agreements appear to replace the current description of activities that might adversely modify habitat that are described under current § 4(b)(8) of the ESA, which the bill would repeal. Those descriptions of activities are necessarily general. Under the new language, the Secretary would have to respond to many individual landowners within 90 days, which could require large resources. Landowners might seek such agreements in lieu of submitting conservation plans. One consequence is specified if the Secretary does not respond within the 90-day period.

Tax Incentives

Related provisions that would provide various tax incentives to persons who execute conservation agreements are contained in a companion Senate bill, S. 1181. The tax advantages would relate to conservation agreements that evidently would be different form those authorized under S. 1180. Whether some of the agreements authorized under S. 1180 could coincidentally qualify for the tax incentives is not clear.

H.R. 2351

The House bill contains fewer provisions on habitat conservation agreements than does the Senate bill. For example, it does not contain safe harbor provisions or habitat reserve agreements.

Definitions

Section 101 of the bill (p. 5) would redefine the term "critical habitat" in § 3(5) of the ESA. The current definition begins by stating that the term critical habitat "means…", while the new definition would begin that the term critical habitat "includes…," thereby making the definition more open-ended. However, it would eliminate the final portion of the subsection. The eliminated subparagraphs currently state, respectively, that critical habitat may be established for species for which it was not established previously, and that critical habitat would not usually include the entire geographical area which can be occupied by the listed species. The first action may simply eliminate a basically unnecessary provision. The elimination of the second provision, combined with the change from "means' to "includes" arguably would allow more generous critical habitat designations that could encompass the entire geographical area which can be occupied by the listed species. The first action may simply eliminate a basically unnecessary provision. The elimination of the second provision, combined with the change from "means" to "includes" arguably would allow more generous critical habitat designations that could encompass the entire geographical area a species could occupy. This could result in more frequent § 7 consultations and possibly in a broader reach of the term "harm," in that it may be easier to show that destruction of habitat actually kiss or injures species if the habitat has been designated as critical.

Other definitions also would affect habitat. "Cumulative impacts" would be defined (pp. 6-7) as those direct and indirect impacts on a species or its habitat that result from the incremental impact of the proposed action when added to other past, present, and reasonably foreseeable future actions, regardless of what person undertakes such other actions. "Impacts" is defined, for purposes of the preceding definition, as 'including' the loss of individual members of the species or "diminishment of the species' habitat, both qualitatively and quantitatively." There are no limiting words with respect to the diminishment of habitat. Another element of impacts would be "disruption of normal behavioral patterns, including but not limited to breeding, feeding, or sheltering..." This language is similar to part of the definition of "harm" in current regulations,[23] but is more far-reaching in that there is no indication of any threshold level of disruption that must be found.

Direct and indirect impacts also are defined. Direct impacts would be those that are caused by the proposed action and that occur at the same time and place. Indirect impacts would be those that are caused by the proposed action and that occur later in time than, or farther removed in distance form the proposed action, but that are still reasonably foreseeable. Read together, these new defined terms could encompass a broad spectrum of actions. The import of this depends on the context in which the terms are used. In some provisions, the terms are used in connection with required studies and this may or may not constitute a significant burden. In other instances, as will be discussed the definitions are also relevant to required actions. For example, new § 19(a)(2), would require an applicant to analyze, minimize and mitigate individual and cumulative impacts, and these requirements could be extensive.

Another term that would affect habitat is the new definition of "recovery" as meaning that the threats to a species as analyzed under section (4)(a) of the ESA "have been eliminated," the species has achieved long-term viability, and the protective measures under this Act are no longer needed. The threats referred to in § 4(a) of the ESA include the "present or threatened destruction, modification, or curtailment of its habitat or range." What is meant by the requirement that this threat be "eliminated" is unclear. A literal reading of this language suggests that *all* destruction, modification, or curtailment of a species' habitat be eliminated in

---

[23] *See* 50 C. F.R. § 17.3, *supra,* which requires that disruption of normal behavioral patterns actually kill or injure wildlife to constitute harm.

order to find the species recovered. This standard could be extremely difficult to meet.

Designation of Critical Habitat; Interim Habitat

Section 102 addresses designation of critical habitat and "survival habitat" (pp. 9-11). Section 4 of the ESA would be amended to require the Secretary, concurrently with listing, to designate "interim habitat" for a species. A new definition of "interim habitat" would also be added as new § 3(28) (p. 9). This term is defined as including "the habitat necessary to support either current populations of a species or populations that are necessary to ensure survival, whichever is larger." Because this definition again uses an "includes" format, it may encompass other habitat as well. Interim habitat could be characterized as survival habitat, and critical habitat could be characterized as recovery habitat. Designation of interim habitat would be based only on biological factors, with special consideration for currently occupied habitat. Interim habitat would be replaced by critical habitat when a final recovery plan was adopted. There appear to be no regulatory consequences to an area (federal or not) being designated as interim habitat, because that habitat is not related to other provisions of the Act; there are no requirements for consultation, conference, avoidance of jeopardy, etc. Instead, it appears that this designation merely informs the public that the designated areas are important to the species.

Section 102 (p. 109) would eliminate the options in current law § 4(a)(3) to omit critical habitat designation where it is not "prudent" (e.g., when theft of organisms is a significant conservation problem) or to delay it for 1 year when critical habitat is not determinable. It would do so by eliminating both options. The FWS or NMFS could address the problem of theft or wanton destruction once the listed species' most important habitats have been published in the *Federal Register*. For certain marine species, critical habitat need be designated only "to the maximum extent biologically determinable…" As current law provides, areas may be excluded from critical habitat on economic grounds, but § 102 (p. 10) amends ESA's §4(b)(2) so that the exclusion could occur only if it did not "impair the species' recovery", a more stringent standard than under current law. Like S. 1180, it would require (in §102, p. 9) critical habitat to be designated at the time the recovery plan was issued.

Basis for Incidental Take Permits

Section 108 of the bill (p. 23) addresses permits and consideration plans and would make certain changes to the current § 10 provisions. Current § 10(a)(1)(A) on permits to do otherwise prohibited acts for scientific and other purposes, and

(B) on incidental take permits would be retained. These current provisions make it clear that § 10 allows acts and takings that would otherwise be prohibited by § 9. New language would be added to subsection (a)(1), and hence apparently apply to both scientific and incidental take situations, to direct the Secretary to limit the duration of a permit "as necessary to ensure that changes in circumstances that could occur in the period and that would jeopardize the continued existence of the species are reasonably foreseeable." This provision may meant that a permit should be of short enough duration to make the effects of changed circumstances foreseeable, presumably so that the Secretary can then respond to these circumstances in the provisions of new permits issued thereafter. This provision highlights the difficulty in crafting consideration plans and permits in a way that provides a term that is long enough to assure habitat over time, yet is short enough to respond to changed circumstances.

Under new § 10(a)(2)(A), no permit for incidental take under § 10(a)(1)(B) (concerning incidental takes) could be issued unless the required application and conservation plan was based on "the best scientific and commercial information available." (p. 24). This standard could be difficult and expensive for individuals or small-scale applicants.

Conservation Plan Requirements

New § 10(a)(2)(B) would set out new requirements for consideration *plans* "under this paragraph." Which plans are included here is not clear. Paragraph (a)(2) cross references paragraph (1)(B) on *permits* that allow incidental take. Low effects permits would be included within § 10 (a)(1)(B), yet imposing all the requirements of (a)(2)(B) to those permits and supporting plans arguably would be burdensome. Also, the separate provisions set out in new § 10(a)(2)(C) (p. 26) could be seen as additional requirements for permits (as opposed to plans issued for incidental take. Perhaps this point and the intended relationship between the new requirements of §10 (a)(2)(B) and (a)(2)(C) could be clarified.

In any event, plans would have to include a description of the specific activities to be authorized; a description and analysis of a reasonable range of alternative actions that would avoid takes; the individual and cumulative impacts (see definitions of cumulative impacts), including the impacts of modification or destruction of habitat of species; objective, measurable biological goals to be achieved for each species covered by the plan; conservation measures the applicant will implement to minimize and mitigate the impacts, including conservation measures for achieving the biological goals an any additional requirements, restrictions, or other adaptive management provisions that are necessary to respond to all reasonably foreseeable changes in circumstances that could jeopardize covered species, including new scientific information and changed conditions; the foreseeable costs; monitoring the applicant will perform to assess the effectiveness of the conservation measures in achieving the plan's goals and impacts on recovery of each species; funding; and other matters the Secretary may require.

Because of the breadth of the definitions of terms (such as cumulative impacts as discussed above, pp. 6-7) used here, the requirement to specify the individual and cumulative impacts of proposed activities could be quite extensive. Arguably an applicant would have to analyze any diminishment of habitat and any direct or indirect impacts on the species involved and its habitat, whether from the proposed action or from any other reasonably foreseeable actions, regardless of who undertakes the actions. It is not clear what might be encompassed by "actions," which might refer only to human actions rather than natural events. If natural events are included, this requirement could be difficult to meet.

Also, under new § 10(a)(2)(C) (p. 26), the Secretary could not issue a permit under paragraph (1)(b)—on incidental taking—unless the Secretary finds that the plan meets all of the requirements "of this paragraph" (apparently meaning paragraph (2) that cross references incidental take permits) and also "finds" several additional things: the taking will be incidental; the applicant will minimize and mitigate the individual impacts and cumulative impacts of takings; the activities to be authorized are consistent with the recovery of the species and will result in no net loss of value to the species of the habitat occupied by the species; the applicant has filed performance bond or surety to ensure adequate funding for each element of the plan; and the permit will ensure implementation of the conservation plan. The first two requirements are similar to current law; the last three would be new. The requirement in new § 10(a)(2)(C)(iii) that the agreements are to be consistent with recovery and will result in no net loss of habitat value would set a standard for such agreements. How the standard would apply in practice could be problematic in that, arguably, it would be likely to work best in an area where most landowners were participating in order that the burdens not fall disparately on those owners who enter agreements. Here too, the intended applicability to low effect permits could be more clear. (The bonding requirements are discussed below.)

Note that here, as in the requirements for plans, because of the definition of "minimize and mitigate" (p. 8), the emphasis would be on avoiding takes through better design of projects and activities. Also, the activities to be authorized would have to be consistent with the *recovery* of the species and there would have to be no net loss of the value to the species of the habitat occupied by the species.

(Presumably this last language refers to "in the plan area.") There is no elaboration on how the no net loss of habitat value will be determined.

Report Requirements

New § 10(a)(2)(D) (p. 27) would require a permitted to provide to the Secretary "at least every year" a "complete report," which will be made public, on the biological status of the species in the affected area, the impacts of the plan and permitted actions on the species, and whether the biological goals of the plan are being met. There is no threshold requirement for these reports, it is not clear how extensive these "complete" reports must be, and there is no exemption for holders of low effects permits. Arguably, this requirement could be burdensome in the context of low-effect permits. New § 10(q)(3) (p. 28) would direct the Secretary annually to report on the status of permits generally and to review and complete reports on individual permits and conservation plans every 3 years.

Modification of Permits

New § 10(a)(2)(E) (p. 27) addresses the important question of whether and how actions allowed under a § 10 incidental take permit may be modified. The bill expressly would allow the Secretary to require a permittee to implement conservation measures in addition to those specified in the plan if they are necessary to ensure that jeopardy is avoided and if the Secretary pays the costs that are in excess of the reasonably foreseeable costs specified in the plan. Funds to carry out these additional measures would be available under the Habitat Conservation Plan Fund in new § 19(a)(9) (p. 35). Plans and permits would be keyed to being consistent with a recovery plan for the species involved, and this language would allow adjustments to avoid jeopardy should circumstances change so much that jeopardy became a possibility. It is not clear what could be included within "costs" –*e.g.* if a change required trees to be left standing, is the opportunity cost of the lost timber value a "cost" to be covered by the Secretary?

Revocation

New § 10(a)(4) (p. 28-29) would direct the Secretary to revoke a permit issued under § 10 and suspend activities authorized by a permit if a permittee was not in compliance with the terms and conditions of the permit, the ESA, or regulations issued under the ESA, including not "substantially" complying with a conservation plan required for a permit, or exceeding the level of take authorized in a permit. Under new § 10(a)(5), (p.29), if a permittee "defaults" on *any* obligation under a conservation plan or an incidental take permit, the Secretary would be directed to "undertake actions to conserve each species covered by the plan and permit," and may use the proceeds of a performance bond or other financial security for this purpose. Note that the bill language varies as to whether substantial noncompliance is required or whether any failure to comply suffices. Also, it is not clear what the Secretary is to do by way of undertaking actions in this regard, considering that private lands are involved—would the Secretary seek a court order directing that certain actions be performed or not performed, or would the Secretary enter lands to carry out actions? Can the penalty provisions of the ESA be immediately invoked for takes not in accordance with a permit or must a revocation action occur first? The revocation provision applies to all permits issued under § 10, not just to the incidental take permits.

Low-Effect, Small Scale Permits

Like S. 1180. H.R. 2351 contains provisions for an easier permitting process for low-effects projects. A new paragraph (6)(pp. 30-32) would be added to § 10(a) to authorize streamlined application and approval procedures for low-effect, small scale plans and permits. Applicants for these permits would not be required to post bond or provide the financial surety other applicants would. These permits could be issued if the action is expected to be of less than 5 years duration; the plan is applicable to fewer than 5 acres (there is elaboration on this point); the project in question is not part of a larger project with additional impacts; the Secretary determines the plan will have a negligible cumulative and individual impact on the recovery of listed species; and the actions is not related to other action with addition impacts (with elaboration on this point). The Secretary is to monitor the implementation and results of these permits to ensure they do not jeopardize the continued existence of any listed species. If additional measures are needed to avoid jeopardy, the Secretary may require them and pay the costs of their implementation. As noted previously, it is not totally clear whether the requirements of new § 10(a)(2) other than bonding apply to low-effects permits.

The requirement for use of the best scientific and commercial information available seems to apply to low-effect permits, because it applies to all permits allowing take. This requirement could remove much of the advantage of the low-effect permit option.

Monitoring

New § 10(a)(7) (p. 32) would direct the Secretary to monitor all conservation plans to ensure they do not jeopardize the continued existence of a listed species. There is no comparable provision in S. 1180.

Bond Requirements

New § 10(a)(8) (p. 32) would require that, before an incidental take permit is issued, the applicant must post a performance bond payable to the United States and conditioned on faithful performance of the permit, or deposit other forms of financial security of the same or greater value as the bond. The among would be determined by the Secretary, based on mitigation requirements and should be sufficient to complete all conservation measures to be implemented by the permittee. Bond for large-scale plans or for very expensive plans could be in the form of phased bonds or deposits for different parts of the plan. Similarly, bond or security could be released in parts as well, after public notice and a review by the Secretary of whether the plan in question was adequately implemented. Bond would not be required for low-effect, small scale permits. (S. 1180 does not contain bond or surety requirements.)

Habitat Conservation Plan Fund

New § 10(a)(9) (pp. 35-37) would create a Habitat Conservation Plan Fund in the Treasury that would consist of donated funds, appropriations, fees charged for permits, amounts received as natural resource damages under new § 12 of the ESA and proceeds of performance bonds and other security. Monies from the Fund (capped at $20 million annually) would be permanently appropriated and could be used by the Secretary to cover the costs of additional conservation measures necessitated by changed circumstances, additional requirements under paragraph (6) for recovery of a species under a low-effect permit,[24] additional actions taken by the Secretary to conserve species under paragraph (5) upon default of a permittee, certain permitting costs, and restoration or replacement of natural resources with respect to which natural resource damages were paid into the fund.

Multispecies Plans

A new paragraph (10) would be added to § 10(a) (pp. 37-39) to authorize multiple landowner, multispecies planning. The Secretary would be directed to encourage the development of these plans and to cooperate to the maximum extent practicable with states and local governments to streamline permitting processes across jurisdictions. This cooperation could include issuing incidental take permits to states, local governments, or groups of local governments who would then issue incidental take "certificates" to landowners. These certificates

---

[24] New paragraph (6)(p.32) would authorize the Secretary to impose and pay for additional measures under a low effect permit if the measures are necessary to avoid jeopardy to the continued existence of a species. Therefore, the reference here to "recovery" may be incorrect.

appear to be similar to federal incidental take permits. States, local governments, or groups of local governments would have to meet the bond or security requirements, including possibly pooled bonds, with respect to all certificates, or ensure that the landowner to whom the certificate is used meets those requirements. Another requirement would be that the recipient state, etc. ensure that all certificates would be consistent with the permit and approved habitat conservation plan; that the recipient would provide adequate public notice and opportunity to comment; and that the recipient would have adequate authority to enforce the terms and conditions of certificates. The Secretary would be required to ensure broad participation in the development of the plan, to provide technical assistance to the maximum extent practicable, and to give these plans priority consideration for funding under § 6.

Notice; Public Participation

New § 19(a)(11) (pp. 39-40) would require the Secretary to publish a notice in the *Federal Register* and provide a 60-day comment period on all applications for § 10 permits. A notice of permit approval with agency responses to public comments must also be published. These requirements would apply to all § 10 permits, including the low effect/small scale permits.

The Secretary also would be required to publish notice of agency involvement in the development of large-scale conservation plans and invite member of the public to participate in the development of large-scale conservation plans and multiple landowner, multispecies plans. The Secretary would promulgate new regulations to establish a process for development of these plans which ensures an "equitable balance" of participation among citizens with a primary interest in carrying out economic development activities that may affect species conservation and citizens whose primary interest is in species conservation. Meetings of participants would not be subject to the Federal Advisor Committee Act, but would be open to the public. The Secretary would be directed to invite independent scientists (as defined in the bill with respect to recovery plans) with expertise on the relevant species to provide input. A large-scale conservation plan would be defined as one that would cover a significant portion of the range of a threatened species, endangered species, candidate species, or species proposed for listing.

Community Assistance Program

New § 10(a)(12) (p. 42) would direct the Secretary to establish a Community Assistance program to provide information to local governments or property owners. Employees of the Fish and Wildlife Service would be assigned to field offices to provide information on local impacts of listings, recovery planning efforts, and other actions, as well s to provide assistance on obtaining permits and achieving other compliance with the ESA, training federal personnel, and serving as a focal point between federal agencies and property owners and local governments.

Natural Resources Damages

Section 110 of the bill (p. 44-45) provides that persons, who in violation of the ESA, negligently damage any member or habitat of a listed species would be liable to the United States (or to a state under management or cooperative agreements) for the costs incurred in restoring or replacing the member or habitat. Monies received by the United States would be deposited in the Habitat Conservation Plan Fund and could only be obligated for the acquisition or rehabilitation of damaged habitat or populations. It is not clear whether this section dovetails adequately with the wording of the prohibitions in § 9 and the penalties of § 11. The new provision refers to *negligent* damage of habitat, yet both the civil and criminal penalties of § 11 are keyed to persons who "knowingly violate" the Act. Therefore the wording of the new provision, which refers both to negligent actions and to "violation of" the ESA is unclear. If a new type of enforcement action is intended, perhaps a clarified statement of what the prohibited action is and what penalties would apply could be included. The remainder of the new provisions authorize a civil action by the Secretary under the subsection and require notice of the action to the person against whom the action is commenced.

Tax Incentives

Title II of the House bill would provide for various tax incentives to encourage conservation agreements. These agreements apparently would be separate from those authorized in the bill. Whether agreements could be structured to serve both purposes is not clear, but is not specifically prohibited.

CONSULTATION

Current Law

Under current § 7(a)(2) and (3) of the ESA, federal agencies are required to consult with the Secretary of the Interior (acting through the Fish and Wildlife Service) or with the Secretary of Commerce (acting through the National Marine

Fisheries Service) to insure that any action authorized, funded, or carried out by the agency is not likely to jeopardize the continued existence of any endangered or threatened species or result in the destruction or adverse modification of critical habitat of a listed species, unless the agency has been granted an exemption under the Act. In fulfilling the requirements of this paragraph, each agency shall use the best scientific and commercial data available. Because "actions authorized, funded, or carried out" may include private actions that receive federal authorization or funding, § 7 consultations may include private as well as federal actions whenever the private actions have a federal nexus. This fact is expressly acknowledged in § 7(a)(3).

Under § 7(a)(4), agencies are to "confer" (a less formal process) with the Secretary on any agency action which is likely to jeopardize the continued existence of any species proposed to be listed under § 4 or result in the destruction or adverse modification of critical habitat proposed to be designated for such species.

To determine whether consultation is necessary, an agency may ask the Secretary whether listed species might be in the affected area; if so, the action agency conducts a "biological assessment" to determine the presence of species that might be affected by the proposed action. This assessment may be done as part of the preparation of documents under the National Environmental Policy Act (NEPA).

When an agency consults, the Secretary provides the agency and the applicant, if any, a written statement—the biological opinion—detailing how the agency action affects the species or its critical habitat. If jeopardy or adverse modification of critical habitat is found, the Secretary suggests reasonable and prudent *alternatives* to the action, which the Secretary believes can be taken to avoid jeopardy. If the Secretary finds the proposed action will not jeopardize a species and that any takings will be incidental to the agency action, the Secretary will issue a statement that specifies the impacts of such incidental taking and specifies reasonable and prudent *measures* that the Secretary considers necessary or appropriate to minimize impacts. From the time consultation begins, the federal agency and the applicant are not to make any irreversible or irretrievable commitment of resources that could foreclose the formulation of alternatives. In practice, jeopardy opinion result form less than one or two per cent of all consultations and in most cases, alternatives are available that allow the action agency to proceed.

Thus, the consultation process provides for a biological review of agency actions by a separate agency (either FWS or NMFS) though procedures that have been praised by some as an effective protective process and condemned by others as a time-consuming impediment. Proposals for change have ranged from doing away with all outside-agency review to better integration of the consultation process and other environmental reviews with agency planning and decision-making processes to make them run concurrently whenever possible and to shorten the time required for reviews. The success of these efforts will depend at least in part on the availability of adequate personnel at the FWS and NMFS. Some observers have asserted that, in addition to or as a substitute for the § 10 permit process, some greater access to consultation would be helpful to private landowners.

S. 1180

Section 4 of the bill addresses interagency consultation and cooperation (pp. 130-142) and would add a definition of "reasonable and prudent alternatives" to § 3 of the ESA that would enact the definition of that phrase that is currently in the regulations. [25] There currently is no statutory definition of this phrase.

Section 4(b) of the bill (p. 131) would add a new § 7 (a)(1)(B) to require each federal agency that is "responsible for the management of land and water" to conduct an inventory of the presence or occurrence of listed, proposed, and candidate species on its lands. An update of this inventory would be required at least once every 10 years. It is not clear which agencies would be included within this wording of agencies responsible for the management of land and water—*e.g.*, the Department of Defense manages a great deal of land, but that is not its primary mission. If the intent is to apply the provision to less than all agencies that have some responsibility for the management of land and water, Congress may consider so specifying.

When Consultation Required; Streamlined Procedure

It appears that the proposed changes to the current § 7 consultation process would eliminate some, and possibly many, current consultations. Under § 4(c) of the bill (p. 132-134), an agency would notify the Secretary if *the agency* determines that an action may affect a listed species or critical habitat. The agency would consult on actions unless the agency determines, based on the opinion of "a qualified biologist" that the action is not likely to adversely affect a listed species or critical habitat, notifies the Secretary of that determination, provides the information on which the agency based the determination, and the Secretary does not object t the determination within 60 days after notice is received. This process

---

[25] 50 C. F. R. § 402.02.

would appear to allow greater scope for agency reviews, yet preserve the opportunity for the Secretary to intervene if there is disagreement about the likely effects of the action. However, several points can be noted. Under current regulations, either the agency or the FWS may initiate conferencing or consultation.[26] Under the new language, the agency in question would make the initial decision on which the subsequent steps are premised. If an agency chooses not to notify the Secretary that an action "may affect" species, there is no stated recourse for the Secretary to intervene, and the agency decision may not be reviewable under a citizen suit provision.

The possibility that the Secretary might not be able to intervene would be at least partially offset by the provision allowing the Secretary to establish categories that would not be subject to the above described agency procedure. Secondly, it is not specified whether the "qualified biologist" must be an agency employee. Third, there is no qualifying language (*e.g.,* "best scientific or commercial data available") as to the type of information on which the agency may rely to determine that the proposed action is not likely to adversely affect listed species. In addition, having agency determinations prevail unless a politically appointed official (rather than non-agency biologists) intervenes, arguably could allow more actions to go forward than is true under the current system.

New § 7(a)(3)(B)(iii) (p. 134) would authorize the Secretary to identify categories of actions that *are* likely to have an adverse effect on species and for which the streamlined agency determination procedures described above would not apply.

New § 7(a)(3)(B)(iv) sets out the grounds on which the Secretary could object to agency determinations that consultations are not needed. The Secretary could object (and thereby force regular consultation) if: the Secretary determines that the action may have an adverse effect on an endangered or threatened species or critical habitat; the Secretary finds there was insufficient information to support the agency's determination; or the Secretary finds that review cannot be completed within the 60 day limit. The Secretary also is to report to Congress on implementation of the agency consultation provisions.

Participation of Applicants

New § 7(a)(30(c) (p. 135) and new § 7(b)(1)(D) (pp. 139-141) would allow applicants to participate in the consultation process by submitting and discussing information on the effects of a proposed action and on reasonable and prudent alternatives, and to receive information on that used by the Secretary in

---

[26] 50 C. F. R. §§ 402.10 and 402.14.

developing a draft and final biological opinion. An applicant may also receive a copy of a draft biological opinion and discuss the basis of any of its findings. The Secretary would be required to explain to the applicant why any alternatives suggested by the applicant were not included in the opinion. All comments and other information submitted to or received from an applicant would be maintained and made available to the public. Compliance with these provisions could provide opportunities for extensive input from applicants; but could entail a significant level of agency response.

GAO Report

Under § 4(d) of the bill (p. 136). The General Accounting Office would be required to report to certain committees of Congress on the costs of formal consultation to the federal agencies and other persons, including the costs of reasonable and prudent measures imposed.

Consultation on Federal Land Plans

Section 4(e) of the bill (pp. 136-138) would add a new § 7(a)(5) to address what consultation must occur on the land management plans of the Forest Service and the Bureau of Land Management when new species are listed. The new language would include such plans within the term "action," and then impose deadlines on consultations that may be required "on an already approved actions as defined under subparagraph (A)..." However, because "action," would be defined in the bill as "including" plans, the special provisions on reinitiation of consultations in the land planning context could be interpreted as applying to other actions as well.[27] As drafted, new § 7(a)(5)(B) is not limited to reinitiation of consultation on the *plans* referred to in subparagraph (A).

During the time of a reinitiated consultation, an agency may go forward with a site-specific, ongoing or previously scheduled action within the scope of a plan if consultation is not required; or if consultation is required, the Secretary issues a biological opinion and the action satisfies the requirements "of this section [§ 7]."

Consolidated Consultation

A new § 7(a)(6) (p. 138) would statutorily authorize certain consultation consolidation practices. With the approval of the Secretary, consultation and conferencing between the Secretary and an agency could include a number of related or similar actions by the agency to be carried out within a particular geographic area. Similarly, the Secretary would be authorized to consolidate

---

[27] *See* the definition of "action" in 50 C.F.R. § 402.02.

requests for consultation or conferencing from various agencies that might affect the same listed or proposed species within an area.

State Information

In conduction consultations, new § 7(b)(1)(C) would direct the Secretary to actively solicit and consider information from the state agency in each affected state. "State agency" is currently defined in § 3(18) of the ESA as any state governmental entity responsible for the management and conservation of fish, plant or wildlife resources in a state.

Reasonable and Prudent Measures

When the Secretary issues a written statement under § 7(b)(4) specifying incidental taking allowed as a result of consultation, the current reference to including specific reasonable and prudent measures that the Secretary considers necessary or appropriate to "minimize" (p. 141). Additionally, new language would be added to state that reasonable and prudent measures "shall be related both in nature and extent to the effect of the proposed activity that is the subject of the consultation."

Emergency Consultation Deferrals

After current ESA § 7(p) which addresses emergency actions in disaster areas, § 4(j) of the bill (p. 142) would add a new subsection § 7(q) to allow consultation to be deferred in response to a natural disaster "or other emergency" for the emergency repair of a natural gas pipeline, hazardous liquid pipeline, or electrical transmission facility, if the repair is necessary to address an imminent threat to human lives or an imminent and significant threat to the environment. Consultation would be required to be initiated as soon as practicable after the threat was abated.

H.R. 2351

Section 107 of the House bill (pp. 16-22) would approach consultation issues by changing certain standards, expanding public participation, and by streamlining some procedures.

Consultations on Candidate and Proposed Species

New § 7(a)(5) (p.17) would allow a federal agency to consult on actions that might affect candidate or proposed species. Under current regulations, an agency may confer (the less formal process) on actions likely to affect proposed species, but there is no opportunity for formal consultation regarding species proposed for listing and no opportunity for conferring or consulting on candidate species.[28] If an agency consults on proposed or candidate species under the new provisions, there would be no need to re-consult if the species is later listed, unless there is significant new information that was not considered in the original consultation or a significant change in the agency proposal. A federal agency would be required to notify the Secretary of any significant change in or significant new information regarding any action on which there was pre-listing consultation.

Monitoring

Under new § 7(a)(6) (p. 18), each federal agency would be required to monitor the status and trends of endangered, threatened and candidate species on lands or in water under the administration of the agency.

Biological Opinions

Section 107(b) of the bill (P. 18) would amend the current § 7(b) provisions on the biological opinion to include a cross-reference to the early consultations and to direct the Secretary to describe the amount of habitat and the number of members of the species that would be taken, together with conservation actions to minimize and mitigate the impacts of any incidental taking that may result from the action. New § 7(b)(5) would require the Secretary would also briefly describe the proposed agency action and to make available information concerning the consultation. Under new § 7(b)(6), in preparing a § 7 opinion, the Secretary would invite independent scientists with expertise on affected species to provide input into the consultation or biological opinion. The term "independent scientist" would have the same meaning given the term in new § 4(f)(1)(D) on listing. Upon completion of a written statement (biological opinion), the Secretary would publish the Secretary's findings and reasoning in the *Federal Register*.

Standard for Allowing Takes

New § 7(b)(4) (P. 20) would change the standard for when the Secretary may allow takes following § 7 consultation. Under current law, the Secretary must find only that the taking of listed species will not violate the subsection on avoiding jeopardy. This language would be changed to require that the incidental takings "will not interfere with the timely achievement of recovery goals." This would be a stricter standard.

---

[28] 50 C.F.R. § 402.10.

Reasonable and Prudent Measures

Other new requirements would be added with respect to incidental takes. The Secretary would specify reasonable and prudent measures that both minimize *and mitigate* impacts. (This same change is proposed in S. 1180 in § 4(i) of the bill (p. 141).) Agencies that were allowed to incidental takes would also be required to assess and report to the Secretary on the amount of incidental take that occurred as a direct impact, indirect impact, or cumulative impact. Again, because of the breadth of the definitions of terms relating to impacts, this reporting arguably could be extensive. If an assessment indicated that the amount of incidental take exceeded that authorized under the written statement, the agency would immediately have to reinitiate consultation.

Under § 107(c) of the bill (p. 21), new § 7(c)(1) would require that agency biological assessments be made available to the public.

Consultations on Foreign Activities

Under § 107(d) of the bill (p. 21), a new § 7(q) would be added to require that § 7 apply to any agency action (which apparently would include private actions with federal authorization or funding) with respect to listed, proposed, or candidate species "carried out in whole or in part, in the United States, in a foreign country, or on the high seas." This would resolve an important question on the scope of the ESA and would greatly expand its application. For example, projects carried out through the Agency for International Development or the Department of Defense might trigger consultation or conferencing with the FWS or NMFS. It is not clear whether negotiations on trade agreements might also be subject to ESA scrutiny.

Consolidated Consultations

A new § 7(r)(pp. 21-22) would require that within a year after enactment the Secretary "in cooperation with the States" to promulgate regulations to ensure timely conclusion of consultations. These regulations should include, to the extent practicable and if approved by the Secretary, consolidation of similar or related agency actions to be undertaken within a particular geographical range or ecosystem, and, to the extent practicable, consolidated requests from various federal agencies involving actions and species that are dependent on the same ecosystem. "Ecosystem" would be defined for purposes of this subsection. Aside form the references to ecosystems (rather than merely to geographical areas), these provisions are very similar to those of S. 1180 (p. 138).

INCENTIVES FOR PRIVATE LANDOWNERS

Incentives for landowners can be loosely divided into several types: (a) tax incentives; (b) direct payments or compensation; (c) public recognition for the outstanding efforts of persons outside the federal government to conserve listed species; and (d) increased certainty about future regulatory requirement. Current law provides no tax incentives, and direct payments, if any, are not included in the ESA itself. For direct compensation, if a landowner feels that a "taking" of property rights in the Constitutional sense has occurred, the remedies are simply those available to any citizen whose property rights have been taken under any other laws. There has been little, if any, direct compensation for property takings under the ESA, because findings of takings meeting Fifth Amendment standards have been rare. The ESA contains no formal mechanism for public recognition, though some agency events have recognized persons making exceptional contributions to conservation of listed species.

Tax benefits have not been a common approach to landowner incentives. The drawbacks appears not to be with the approach so much as with multiple committee referrals and an intense concern about eliminating the deficit. As a result, supporters of tax incentives often segregate such provisions into separate bills. In the 105th Congress, for example, S. 1181 would offer extensive tax benefits for persons carrying out conservation activities for listed species on private lands. No action has occurred on this bill.

The burden of providing incentives under current law has fallen almost entirely to increasingly certainty about future regulatory requirements and associated relief from those requirements. Under the direction of Secretary Babbitt, FWS has offered certain regulatory incentives to private landowners. The incentives address management of land on which listed species already exist (*no take agreements, no surprises, safe harbor), and land where the species is not yet found (safe harbor)*. Many who approve of these approaches would like to see them made permanent law, rather than subject to the changing policies of successive secretaries.

The duration of such agreements is hotly debated. On the one hand, they can lock in a landowner to carry out specified conservation measures for decades, at a level that might not be achieved otherwise. They may also turn former antagonists into cooperators, thereby speeding the implementation of conservation measures or reducing landowners' incentives to eliminate organisms or their habitat in the period before a listing becomes effective. On the other hand, if a Habitat Conservation Plan (or other agreements under ESA) is inadequate to meet its conservation goals from the start, or if a greater understanding of the data later leads to the conclusion that the HCP was inadequate, or if new events lead to greater peril to the covered species the options available to the Secretary to modify the plan could be limited.

S. 1180

Tax Incentives
S. 1180 contains no tax incentives; a companion bill, S. 1181, introduced by Sen. Kempthorne, contains numerous financial incentives for landowners, including tax incentives.

Direct Payments
Current law offers no direct financial incentives to private landowners to augment populations of listed species on their lands. S. 1180 (§3(b), p. 104), would create an entirely new § 5 in the ESA dealing with recovery planning. In a new § 5(1)(4) (p. 119), the Secretary would be authorized to provide grants up to $25,000 to private landowners to implement a recovery plan. The money would be directed to actions that are beyond those necessary to get a permit under ESA or other federal law. For example, owners might seek sport to attract an endangered bird to begin to nest on their property in some area critical to the implementation of an HCP, whose terms and conditions are a requirement for obtaining an incidental take permit. Also S. 1180 (§ 5(f), p. 153) would create a new § 10(1)(3)(A); under it, a landowner participating in a safe harbor agreement would be eligible for a grant up to $10,000. (All grants would be subject to availability of appropriated funds.)

No Surprises Policy
Under a "no surprises" policy, a person who enters into and continues to comply with an HCP would not be required to carry out any additional measures for species covered in the plan if the additional measures would cost the landowner money or result in further restrictions on use of the property. The no surprises policy could be a significant incentive in some situations. S. 1180 (§5 (c), p. 148, creating a new §10 (a)(5)), would require that all HCPs have a "no surprises policy." Such provisions are common but not required in current HCPs. The new provision also states that the HCP must identify other measures that might be required of the applicant under extraordinary circumstances. It does not specify who would fund additional measures should the extraordinary circumstances included in the HCP arise. It places no limits on the duration of the HCPs.

Safe Harbor Agreements

Under current law, landowners who increase suitable habitat and allow listed species to increase their populations levels on their land, or who allow listed species to visit or become established on the land, may see that increase or establishment as a liability or a threat. Many landowners fear increased government regulations, intrusion, or just "hassle." Some may even try to take steps to prevent individuals of a species from residing on their land. In addition, some landowners may try to eliminate a species from their land in anticipation of listing. Although such actions would be legal with respect to unlisted species, recovery could be made more difficult if the species were listed later.

S. 1180 (§ 5(f), p. 153) would amend § 10 of the ESA by adding a new subsection (1). Under the proposal, the Secretary would be allowed to enter into agreements with landowners, under which landowners would still be required to meet the current law's prohibition on taking those listed organisms already present (the "baseline"), but would be allowed to take listed plants or animals without penalty if they reach population levels above the baseline. The Secretary may provide appropriated fund to assist landowners in augmenting listed populations on their lands. There is no limitation on the duration of these agreements.

H.R. 2351

Tax Incentives

Under § 201 of H. R. 2351, landowners who enter into "Endangered Species Conservation Agreements" would be eligible for special tax benefits defined in the Title II (p. 45). Section 202 (p. 39) of the bill would amend Chapter 11 of the tax code (adding a new § 2057) to allow the value of the land covered by the agreement to be deducted from the value of the estate for inheritance taxes. IF the agreement were terminated or the owner disposed of the property, an additional tax would recapture the tax benefit. In addition, the tax code would be amended by § 203 (p. 55) to allow a federal deduction for 25% of the value of state or local property taxes on land covered under one of these agreements.

H.R. 2351 (§204, p. 56) also would provide a credit against the income tax for an amount equal to the costs of the agreement paid or incurred by the taxpayer during the taxable year. These costs would be defined as those expenses that would not have been incurred by the taxpayer but for compliance with the agreement. There would be restriction specified on the size of the credit. Since the provision would provide a credit rather than a deduction, the tax benefits to the landowner could provide a very substantial incentive to participate in these agreements.

Direct Payments
H.R. 2351 does not offer financial incentives beyond the tax incentives.

Safe Harbor Agreements
The bill would codify the "no surprises" policy in that an effort would be made to include provisions in a conservation agreement for reasonably foreseeable circumstances that might necessitate modifications of the 10(a)(2)(B)(v)(II), (p. 25.) In addition, changes could be made if necessary to avoid jeopardy, but these changes would be at the expense of the government. (New § 10(a)(2)(E), pp. 27-28.)

No Surprise Agreements
The bill would codify the "no surprises" policy in that an effort would be made to include provisions in a conservative agreement for reasonably foreseeable circumstances that might necessitate modifications of the activities otherwise allowed under the agreement. (Section 108 adding new § 10(a)(2)(B)(v)(II), p. 25.) In addition, changes could be made if necessary to avoid jeopardy, but these changes would be at the expense of the government. (New § 10(a)(2)(E), pp. 27-28.)

ENFORCEMENT

S. 1180

Section 3(c) of the bill would amend § 11 (g)(1)(C) of the Act to allow citizen suits Against *the Secretary* for failing to perform any nondiscretionary act or duty under new § 5 on recovery plans. This language does not appear to encompass actions related to recovery plans that a state might be authorized to complete. The principal remedy in that case appears to be the authority for the secretary to remove the authority provided a state to develop a plan. A citizen suit might be available to force the Secretary to take this action some circumstances. As discussed above, judicial review of recovery implementation agreements negotiated with a federal agency would be circumscribed and the extent of any review that would be available is unclear. These agreements also apparently could include actions by non-federal parties that receive federal approval or funding.

Section 6 of S. 1180 (pp. 162-163) would add provisions on enforcement actions involving incidental takings. A new subsection (h) would be added to § 11 of the ESA to specify that he Secretary or the Attorney General must provide evidence "based on scientifically valid principles" that the acts of a person "caused" incidental takings. Similar language would be added to the citizen suit provisions of the ESA in § 11(g). This language appears intended to focus on the element of causation in the taking—that the person accused of an incidental taking must be shown to have caused the taking of a listed species. It is not clear whether the language may also affect the level of intent of the part of an accused that is required for enforcement actions. A taking is "incidental to otherwise lawful activity" if the harm or death to a listed species is unintended and happens only incidentally as part of otherwise lawful actions that are the intended acts.

A major change under S. 1180 would be the emphasis on protecting endangered and threatened species through the various types of agreements that would be authorized. The act would authorize multiple species agreements; candidate agreements; safe harbor agreements; no surprise provisions; habitat reserves; and no taking agreements. Potentially, there could be so many of these agreements as to present very real oversight and enforcement problems for the agencies involved. Often these are the circumstances in which citizen suits have been looked to in other contexts to assist with enforcement. However, the various agreements that would be created by the bill do not appear to be enforceable under the current citizen suit provisions of § 11(g) and no new language addressing this issue would be added. Section 11(g) currently allows a person to enjoin another person who is alleged to be in violation of the Act or regulation; or to compel the Secretary to apply certain prohibitions with respect to takings; or against the Secretary for failing to perform any § 4 *non-discretionary* duty. These provisions might not permit citizen suits to enforce the terms of agreements authorized under the new legislation. IF only the federal government can enforce the agreements and if the agreements become numerous, arguably enforcement may become difficult. On private lands, there may also be problems of proof in demonstrating violation of agreements.

Under § 5(c) of S. 1180 (p. 149), a new paragraph (6) would be added to § 10(a) of the ESA to authorize the Secretary to revoke any permits for excused takes *issued under subsection (a)* after notice and an opportunity for correction. It is not clear whether a permittee could be charged with § 9 takings during the time allowed for correction of noncompliance, or whether a permittee could only be charged after permit revocation. The revocation provision would apply to all the types of agreements issued under § 10(a) of the Act, but would not appear to apply to similar agreements placed outside § 10(a) such as the safe harbor agreements and possibly the candidate species agreements. Candidate species agreements would be a new subsection (k) to § 10, which placement would seem to indicate the revocation provisions would not apply to them. However, candidate permits would be cross-referenced in § 10(a)(1), so possibly the revocation provisions were meant to apply. If the revocation provisions do not apply, this would raise the question of what recourse and remedies might be available to the Secretary for non-compliance with the terms of candidate agreements.

H.R. 2351

The House bill would amend § 11(g) to expressly include suit against persons alleged to be in violation of "this Act, any regulation or permit issued under this Act, any statement provided by the Secretary under § 7(b)(3), or *any agreement concluded under authority of this Act.*" Other provisions in the House bill would expand the circumstances in which a plaintiff could proceed with suit on an emergency basis to cover all types of citizen suits and waive the usual 60-day notice of intent to sue. Under current law, an emergency suit may only be brought against the Secretary for failure to perform a non-discretionary duty. Under new § 11(g)(2)(A)(i) and (g)(2)(B)(i) of H.R. 2351 (p. 43) a suit to enjoin any person or to compel the Secretary to apply prohibitions of the Act with respect to takings could also be brought on an emergency basis.

New § 10(a)(4) (p. 28-29) would direct the Secretary to revoke a permit issued under § 10 and suspend activities authorized by a permit if a permittee is not in compliance with the terms and conditions of the permit, the ESA, or regulations issued under the ESA, including not "substantially" complying with a conservation plan required for a permit, or exceeding the level of take authorized in a permit. Under new § 10(a)(5), (p. 29), if a permittee "defaults" on *any* obligation under a conservation plan or an incidental take permit, the Secretary is directed to "undertake actions to conserve each species covered by the plan and permit," and may use the proceeds of a performance bond or other financial security for this purpose. The bill language varies as to whether substantial noncompliance is required or whether any failure to comply suffices. Also, it is not clear what the Secretary is to do by way of undertaking actions in this regard, considering that private lands are involved—would the Secretary seek a court order directing that certain actions be performed or not performed, or would the Secretary enter lands to carry out actions? Can the penalty provisions of the ESA be immediately invoked for takes not in accordance with a permit or must a revocation action occur first? Note too, that the revocation provision applies to all permits issued under § 10, not just to the incidental take permits.

FUNDING NEEDS

The current law and its administration has generated a certain commonality on at least one issue among many of its critics from both the environmental and business communities: some of its problems might be eased with greater funding. Nearly all environmentalists would probably support more monitoring and faster development of recovery plans and listing decisions. Some business interests might like to see faster responses on basic questions about whether a particular project has an ESA conflict, and greater efforts to remove a species and therefore to remove it as a source of delay. Representatives of both groups therefore have supported greater funding in order to achieve these ends, while simultaneously trying to amend the law in markedly different ways. (However, consensus on this goal is greater among environmental groups than business interests.)

Thus, the funding questions are not only the authorization levels, but the burden on the agencies (FWS and NFMS) to work under new regulations, the amount of staff time required to implement the new provisions, and whether appropriations levels would met the demands of new law's more far-reaching provisions.

S. 1180

The bill (§8, p. 166) would set authorizations as shown in Table 1.

Table 1. Authorization Levels under S. 1180, FY1999-FY2003
(in millions of dollars)

	1998	1999	2000	2001	2002	2003
Interior	90	120	140	160	165	165
Commerce	35	50	60	65	65	70
Agriculture	4	4	4	4	4	4
Endangered Species Committee	0.6	0.6	0.6	0.6	0.6	0.6
CITES	1	1	1	1	1	1
Safe harbor-DOI*	10	10	10	10	10	10
Safe harbor-DOC*	5	5	5	5	5	5
HCP loans*	10	10	10	5	5	5
Rec. Ass't DOI	30	30	30	30	30	30
Rec. Ass't DOC*	15	15	15	15	15	15
Total	200.6	245.6	275.6	295.6	300.6	305.6
HC Insurance*	5%	5%	5%	5%	5%	5%

Program marked "*" would be created in the bill. See text for explanations.

H.R. 2351

This bill (§301, p. 58) would set the authorized levels shown in Table 2. The "Cooperative Agreements" shown in the table appear to be identical to the current Cooperative Endangered Species Conservation Fund, which is now authorized, not at a specific amount, but rather as a percent of 2 permanently appropriated funds within the FWS budget. (The current program does not take money from these accounts; their levels are merely markers to set the size of the program.) Amending the current law to authorize specific funding levels and eliminating the provisions in the current law tying this program to the other FWS programs, might clarify this situation.

Table 2. Authorization Levels under H.R. 2351, FY1999-FY2002
(in millions of dollars)

	1999	2000	2001	2002
Interior	130	135	140	145
Commerce	30	35	40	45
CITES	3	3	4	4
HCP Fund*	20	20	20	20
Cooperative agreements-Interior	20	20	20	20
Cooperative agreements-Commerce	5	5	5	5
Total	208	218	229	239

Programs marked "*" would be created in the bill. See text for explanations.

APPENDIX 1. MAJOR PROVISIONS OF
THE CURRENT LAW: DOMESTIC

The ESA (16 U.S.C. §§ 1531-1544) was passed in 1973, but was preceded by simpler acts in 1966 and 1969. It has been amended on numerous occasions since then: 1976, 1977, 1978, 1979, 1980, 1982, and 1988. The following are its major domestic provisions in the order they appear in the U.S. Code. Numbers in parentheses refer to U.S. Code. Numbers in parentheses refer to U.S. Code citations, followed by relevant section or section numbers from the Act.

An **endangered species** is defined as "any species which is in danger of extinction throughout all or a significant portion of its range..." A **threatened species** is defined as "any species which is likely to become an endangered species within the foreseeable future throughout all or a significant portion of its range." The ESA does not rely on a numerical standard: such a standard would not reflect the wide variety of many species' biology. (For example, a population of 10,000 butterflies all confined to one mountaintop, would clearly be at greater risk than 10,000 butterflies scattered over thousands of square miles.) The protection of the Act extends to all species and subspecies of animals (not just birds and mammals), although for vertebrates, further protection can be given even for distinct population segments within a species, and not just the species as a whole. More limited protection is available for plant species under the Act. (16 U.S.C. § 1532, ESA § 3).

The term "take" under the Act means to "harass, harm, pursue, hunt, shoot, wound, kill, trap, capture, or collect, or to attempt to engage in any such conduct." (16 U.S.C. §1532, ESA § 3). (Harassment and harm are further defined in regulation at 50 C.F.R. § 17.3) Taking is prohibited under 16 U.S.C. § 1538. There has been controversy over the extent to which the prohibition on taking may include habitat modification. A 1995 Supreme Court decision (*Sweet Home)* held that the inclusion of significant habitat modification was a reasonable interpretation of the term "harm" in the law.

Most listed species are managed by the Secretary of the Interior through FWS. However, marine species, including some marine mammals, are the responsibility of the Secretary of Commerce, acting through the National Marine Fisheries Service (NMFS). The law assigns the major role to the Secretary of the Interior (all references to "Secretary" below are to the Secretary of the Interior unless otherwise stated) and provides in detail for the relationship of the two Secretaries and their respective powers. (16 U.S.C. § 1533, § 3)

When the appropriate Secretary initiates or receives a substantive petition from a party (which may be a state or federal agency—including FWS or NMFS—an individual, or some other entity), the Secretary must decide whether to list the species, based only on the best scientific information and trade statistics, and after an extensive series of procedural steps to ensure public participation and the collection of information. The Secretary *may not take into account the economic effects that listing may have on the area* where the species occurs. This is the only place in the ESA where economic considerations are expressly forbidden. Some steps may be skipped for emergency listings. Economic factors are not taken into account at this stage because Congress felt that listing was fundamentally a scientific question: is the continuation of the species threatened or endangered? Through the 1982 amendments particularly, Congress clearly intended to separate this scientific question from subsequent decisions on appropriate protection. (16 U.S.C. § 1533, § 4(b))

In the interval between a proposal and a listing decision, the Secretary must monitor the status of these "candidate" species and promptly list them to prevent sudden significant risks (16 U.S.C. § 1533). Furthermore, federal agencies must confer with the appropriate Secretary on actions likely to jeopardize the continued existence of the species proposed to be listed. However, the agencies are not required, for candidate species, to avoid irretrievable commitments of resources. (16 U.S.C. § 1536, § 4(b))

If a species is listed, the Secretary must designate critical habitat (either where the species is found or, if it is not found there, where there are features essential to its conservation) at the time of listing. However, if the publication of this information is not "prudent" because it would harm the species (e.g., by encouraging vandals or collectors), the Secretary may decide not to designate critical habitat. The Secretary may also postpone designation for up to one year if the information is not determinable. (16 U.S.C. § 1533, § 4(b)(6).) As a practical matter, critical habitat has not been designated for the great majority of listed species. While any area, whether or not federally owned, may be designated as critical habitat, private land is affected by designation only if some federal action (e.g., license, loan, permit, etc.) is involved. In either case, federal agencies must avoid "adverse modification" either through their own actions or activities that are federally approved or funded.

The appropriate Secretary must develop recovery plans for the conservation and survival of listed species. Recovery plans to date tend to cover birds and mammals, but a 1988 amendment now forbids the Secretary to favor particular taxonomic groups. (16 U.S.C. § 1533, §4 (f)) The Act and regulations provide little detail on the requirements for recovery plans, no are these plans binding on federal agencies or others.

Land may be acquired to conserve (recover) endangered and threatened species, and money from the Land and Water Conservation Fund may be appropriated for this acquisition. (16 U.S.C. § 1534, § 5)

The appropriate Secretary must cooperate with the states in conserving protected species and must enter into cooperative agreements to assist states in their endangered species programs, if the program meet certain specified standards. If there is a cooperative agreement, the states may receive federal funds to implement the program, but the states must normally provide a minimum 25% matching amount. Under the 1988 amendments, a fund was created to provide for the state grants. While the authorized size of the fund is determined according to a formula, money from the fund still requires annual appropriation. (16 U.S.C. § 1535, § 6).

If their actions may affect a listed species, federal agencies must ensure that those actions (including those affecting private actions such as funding, permit approval, etc.) are "not likely to jeopardize the continued existence" of any endangered or threatened species, nor to adversely modify critical habitat. To be sure of the effects of their actions, they must consult, with the appropriate Secretary. "Action" is quite broadly defined: it includes anything authorized, funded, or carried out by the agency, including permits and licenses. If the appropriate Secretary finds an action would jeopardize the species, he must suggest reasonable and prudent alternatives that would avoid harm to the species. Pending completion of the consultation process, agencies may not make irretrievable commitments of resources that would foreclose any of these alternatives. (16 U.S.C. § 1536, § 7(a)-(d))

Proponents of federal action may apply for an exemption for that action (not for a species) from the Act. Under the ESA, a Committee of six specified federal officials and a representative of each affected state (commonly called the "God Squad") must decide whether to allow a project to proceed despite future harm to a species; at least five votes are required to pass an exemption. The law includes extensive rules and deadlines to be followed in applying for such an exemption and some stringent rules for the Committee in deciding whether to grant an exemption. The Committee must grant an exemption if the Secretary of Defense determines that an exemption is necessary for national security. (16 U.S.C. § 1536, § 7(e)-(p))

For private actions, the Secretary may also issue permits to allow incidental take of species for otherwise lawful actions that do not involve some federal nexus such as loans, permits, licenses, etc. The applicant for an "incidental take permit" must submit a habitat conservation plan (HCP that shows the likely impact, the steps to minimize and mitigate the impact, the funding for the mitigation; the alternatives that were considered and rejected; and any other measures that the Secretary may require. Secretary Babbitt has vastly expanded use of this section, and provided streamlined procedures for activities with minimal impacts. (16 U.S.C. § 1539, § 10(a))

Other provisions specify certain exceptions for raptors; regulate subsistence activities by Alaskan natives; prohibit interstate transport and sale of listed species and parts; control trade in parts or product of an endangered species that were owned before the law went into effect; and specify rules for the establishment of experimental populations among other specialized provisions. (Provisions of the Act referring to international activities are discussed below.) (16 U.S.C. § 1539, § 10(b)-(j))

Prohibited actions are set out and criminal and civil penalties are specified, and provision is made for citizen suits. (16 U.S.C. §§ 1538 and 1540, § 11)

APPENDIX II. MAJOR PROVISIONS OF THE CURRENT LAW: INTERNATIONAL

For the United States, the ESA implements the Convention on International Trade in Endangered Species of Wild Fauna and Flora, ("CITES", TIAS 8249), signed by the United States on March 3, 1973; and the Convention on Nature Protection and Wildlife Preservation in the Western Hemisphere (the "Western Hemisphere Convention"; 50 Stat. 1354; TS 981), signed by the United States on October 12, 1940. CITES parallels the ESA by dividing its listed species into groups, according to the estimated risk of extinction, but uses three major categories, rather than two. In contrast to the ESA, however, CITES focuses exclusively on trade, and does not consider or attempt to control habitat loss. The following are the major international provisions of the ESA:

The Secretary may use foreign currencies (available under 7 U.S.C. § 1691, the Food for Peace program) to provide financial assistance to other countries for conserving endangered species. (As a practical matter, however, very little money is currently available under this provision.) The Act also authorizes appropriations for this purpose. (16 U.S.C. §§ 1537 and 1542, § 8 and § 15)

The Act designates the Interior Secretary as the Endangered Species Scientific Authority (ESSA) under CITES. As the ESSA, the Secretary must determine that export from the United States and import from other countries of living or dead organisms, or their products, will not harm the species in question. The Secretary has authority to enforce these determinations. The Secretary is required to base export determinations upon "the best available biological information," although population estimates are not required. Certain other responsibilities are also spelled out in CITES. (16 U.S.C. §§ 1537-1538, § 8A and § 11)

The Interior Secretary is also named as the Management Authority for the Unite States under CITES. The Management Authority must assure that specimens are exported legally, that imported specimens left the country of origin legally, and that live specimens are shipped under suitable conditions. Certain other responsibilities are also spelled out in CITES. (16 U.S.C. § 1537, § 8A and § 11)

The ESA makes violations of CITES violations of U.S. law if committed within the jurisdiction of the United States. (16 U.S.C. § 1538, § 11).

The ESA requires importers and exporters of controlled products to use certain ports and provides for exemptions for scientific purposes and for programs intended to assist the recovery of listed species. There are also certain exceptions for Alaska Natives and for products owned before December 28, 1973, including scrimshaw. (16 U.S.C. §§ 1538-1539, § 9 and § 10)

Chapter 5

ENDANGERED SPECIES LIST REVISIONS: A SUMMARY OF DELISTING AND DOWNLISTING

Robert J. Noecker

INTRODUCTION

Central the debate before Congress over appropriations for or reauthorization of the Endangered Species ACT (ESA) is the question of whether the Act actually works. Different standards have been used to judge the ESA a failure and a success. Opponents of the Act contend that the ESA has failed while costing taxpayers billions of dollars, citing the low number of "recovered" species removed form the list. Proponents assert that the ESA has succeeded in preserving endangered and threatened species and their habitats, citing the significant number of listed species with stable or increasing populations, or the low number of extinctions of listed species.

Further controversy arises from uncertainty over the definitions for the terms "recovered" and "extinct." Should species that may have been already extinct when listed under the ESA be used to judge the Act's effectiveness? If a species has declined to a point that its very existence is in question, should a later determination that it is in fact extinct be attributed as a failure of the Act? Should species removed from the list because of the discovery of additional populations be classified as "recovered?" Should species downlisted from endangered to threatened due to stable or increasing populations count as "recovered?"

Understanding the process and reasons of removing particular species from the endangered species list, or for reclassifying them from endangered to threatened, will help to answer these questions and to inform the debate.

CHOOSING CRITERIA TO EVALUATE THE ESA

To determine whether the ESA has been effective, one must first choose a standard of measure. The primary goal of the ESA is the recovery of species to levels where protection under the Act is no longer necessary. If this is the standard of measure, the Act could be considered a failure. As of July 31, 1997, only 11 species have been delisted due to recovery. Of the remaining species that have been removed from the endangered and threatened lists, seven have gone extinct, and nine species have been delisted due to new or improved data.

Specifically studies have shown that most species are listed only after there are very deleted (*e.g.,* median population of 999 animals for listed vertebrates, 1075 invertebrates, and 1119.5)[1], and recovery, in the short term, may be unrealistic. Therefore, another standard of measure might be the number of species whose populations have stabilized or increased, even if the species is not actually delisted. Using this standard, the Act could be considered a moderate success, since a large number of the 1,676 listed species (41% according to one study) have improved or stabilized. Twenty-two species originally listed as endangered have been down-listed to threatened status, with two of these eventually being de-listed altogether.

Another standard of measure of the ESA could be the number of species that have not gone extinct. While extinction can be considered a normal evolutionary process, widely diverse methods suggest that current rates of extinction exceed baseline rates by 100-10,000 times. With only 7 of the 1,676 listed species having gone extinct, (although 5 of these were later determined to have been extinct at the tome of listing), this standard could be used to classify the ESA as a success. Species like the California condor and the red wolf might not exist today without ESA protection. On the other hand, less charismatic species at risk may have gone extinct without notice.

In sum, these three different standard would count the ESA as a failure, a modest success or a success. Any participant in the ESA as a failure, a modest

---

[1] Wilcove, Davis S., Margaret McMillan, and Keith C. Winston. What Exactly is an Endangered Species? Analysis of the U.S. Endangered Species List: 1985-1991. Conservation Biology 7(1): 87-93. 1993.

success, or a success. Any participant in the ESA debate could therefore find support for his or her interests by choosing an appropriate standard of measure.

CREATION OF ENDANGERED SPECIES LISTS

Congress first authorized the creation of a federal list of endangered species in the Endangered Species Preservation Act (ESPA) of 1966. As a part of early efforts to halt or reverse the decline of wildlife species, this Act, in part, directed the Secretary of the Interior to publish the names of all species found to be "threatened with extinction" in the *Federal Register (FR)*. The focus of this legislation was the protection of habitat, primarily through federal acquisition. It did not restrict taking or trade in interstate commerce of listed wildlife species.[2]

The Endangered Species Conservation Act (ESCA) of 1969 provided additional protections for declining species. A major innovation was the authorization to create a list of wildlife "threatened with worldwide extinction," and to strictly limit the importation of these species into the United States.[3] The ESCA also directed the Secretary of the interior and the Secretary of State to seek "a binding international convention on the conservation of endangered species."

The Convention on International Trade in Endangered Species of Wild Fauna and Flora (CITES), the result of that congressional call, was signed by 21 nations in 1973 and took effect in 1975. One of its major contributions to endangered species protection was protection was the recognition of different levels of endangerment.[4] CITES listed species on one of three appendices: Appendix I listing the species most vulnerable to extinction; Appendix II listing species less vulnerable, or those species whose trade must be controlled to prevent endangerment; and Appendix III containing species that could be listed unilaterally by countries wishing to prevent over-exploitation of populations within their own boundaries.[5] This agreement was significant both in substantively regulating international trade, and in providing a framework for domestic legislation.

---

[2] Bean, Michael J. *The Evolution of National Wildlife Law.* New York , NY Praeger Publishers, 1983. p. 319-321.

[3] *Ibid.*, p. 321.

[4] *Ibid.*, p. 325.

[5] While the ESA is the domestic legislation implementing many of the provisions of CITES, there is no necessary connection between species' listing on the Appendices of CITES and listing under the ESA.

Congress passed the Endangered Species Act in 1973, replacing both the ESPA and the ESCA. In addition to further restrictions on "taking"[6] and interstate commerce, the ESA authorized the listing of "endangered"[7]and "threatened"[8] wildlife and plants. Those species previously listed under the ESPA and the ESCA were directly incorporated into the Lists of Endangered and Threatened Wildlife and Plants under the ESA, found at 50 CFR § 17.11(h) and § 17.12(h).

PROCESS FOR DELISTING OR DOWNLISTING A SPECIES

The processes for de-listing of down-listing a species from the Lists of Endangered and Threatened Wildlife and Plants are the same as the processes for listing (see Appendix). The Secretary of the Interior may initiate a change in the status of listed species. Alternatively, after receiving a substantive petition for any change in listing status, the Secretary shall conduct a review of the species' status. The determination to delist, downlist, or uplist a species must be made solely on the basis of the best scientific and commercial data available" (ESA, §4(b)(1)(A), "without reference to possible economic or other impacts." (50 CFR §421.11(b)) Fish and Wildlife Service (FWS) regulations also state that, at least once every five years, the Director shall conduct a review of each listed species to determine whether it should be removed from the list (de-listed), changed from endangered to threatened (down-listed), or changed from threatened to endangered (up-listed (50 CFR §424.21).

A species may be removed from the list only if the data substantiate that it is no longer threatened or endangered for one or more of the following reasons.

- First, the Secretary may declare a species to be **extinct** if, after a sufficient period of time, no individuals of a listed species can be found throughout its historical range, or all individuals of captive populations have died.

---

[6] Section 3(18) of the ESA defines the term "take" to mean "harass, harm, pursue, hunt, shoot, wound, kill, trap, capture, or collect, or to attempt to engage in any such conduct."

[7] Section 3(6) of the ESA defines the term "endangered species" to mean "any species which is in danger of extinction throughout all or a significant portion of its range other than a species of the Class Insecta determined by the Secretary to constitute a pest whose protection under the provisions of this Act would present an overwhelming and overriding risk to man."

[8] Section 3(19) of the ESA defines the term "threatened species" to mean "any species which is likely to become an endangered species within the foreseeable future throughout all or a significant portion of its range."

- Second, the Secretary may determine that a species is **recovered** if the best available scientific and commercial data indicate that it is no longer threatened or endangered, and no longer requires the protections of the ESA.
- Third, the **original data,** or the interpretation of such data, used to list a species as endangered or threatened may have been **in error**. The reason could include discovery of previously unknown populations or habitat, or taxonomic revision of the listed species.

After a species has been removed from the endangered or threatened list due to recovery or an effort in the original data, the FWS will continue to monitor its status to insure that proper action has been taken. Emergency re-listing may occur if these monitoring efforts show that the species is again endangered or likely to become endangered (50 CFR §424.20).

EXTINCT SPECIES

Of the 1,676 species on the Lists of Endangered and Threatened Wildlife and Plants (as of November 30, 1997), seven have been de-listed due to extinction. Four of these species—the Tecopa pupfish, longjaw cisco, blue pike, and Santa Barbara song sparrow—were protected under laws pre-dating the ESA, and therefore were automatically listed under the ESA when it passed in 1973. They were apparently already extinct by 1973, however.

Tecopa Pupfish

The Tecopa pupfish (*Cyprinodon nevadenis*) was first described in 1948 from the outflow streams of the north and south Tecopa Hot Springs, north of Tecopa, California. In 1970, the declining Tecopa pupfish population was listed on both the federal and California endangered species lists due to habitat alteration and introductions of exotic species, primarily bluegill sunfish and mosquito fish. By 1872, the species no longer occurred where the species was first found. Surveys done in 1977 failed to locate any other populations. In 1982, the FWS determined the Tecopa pupfish was extinct and removed it from the endangered species list (47 *FR* 2317).

Longjaw Cisco

The longjaw cisco (*Coregonus alpenae*) was one of several species of deepwater whitefish that was an important part of the smoked fish industry in the Great Lakes. It was known to occur in Lakes Michigan, Huron, and Erie. Extensive over-fishing and increased lake pollution led to a population crash in the first half of the 20th Century. The cisco was further decimated by sea lamprey predation and habitat degradation, and has not been seen in Lakes Huron and Erie since the 19650's. The last collection in Lake Michigan was in 1967, at which time the species was listed as endangered under the ESPA. In 1983, the FWS declared the longjaw cisco extinct and took it off the endangered species list (48 *FR* 39942).

Blue Pike

The blue pike *(Stizostedion vitreum glaucum)* was abundant in the commercial fishery of the Great Lakes. It was historically found in Lakes Erie and Ontario and in the Niagara River. In 1915, population levels began a cycle of extreme fluctuation caused by over-fishing, leading to the eventual collapse in 1958. The FWS listed the pike as endangered under the ESCA in 1970, suggesting that introgressive hybridization with walleye may have caused the final disappearance of the stock. A survey by the Blue Pike Recovery Team in 1977 found no individuals. In 1983, the FWS declared the blue pike extinct and removed it from the endangered species list (48 *FR* 39942).

Santa Barbara Song Sparrow

The Santa Barbara song sparrow (*Melospiza melodia graminea)* is a subspecies of the song sparrow that was known to exist only on Santa Barbara Island, Los Angeles County, California. No Santa Barbara song sparrows have been seen since a fire in 1959 destroyed most of the 640-acre island's habitat. In 1983, the FWS determined that *M. m. graminea* was extinct and removed it from the endangered species list (48 *FR* 46336).

Sampson's Pearly Mussel

Sampson's pearly mussel (*Epioblasma (=Dysnomia) sampsoni*) is a freshwater bivalve mollusk that was historically found in parts of the Wabash River in Illinois and Indiana, and parts of the Ohio River near Cincinnati. Dam construction and siltation eliminated much of the gravel and sandbar habitat where the species was found. The FWS listed this mussel as endangered under the ESA in 1976 (41 *FR* 24064). A status review initiated in 1981 determined that "no specimens have been collected in over 50 years, despite repeated sampling within its range." In 1984, the FWS concluded that Sampson's pearly mussel was extinct and removed it from the endangered species list (49 *FR* 1057).

Amistad Gambusia

The Amistad gambusia (*Gambusia amistadensis*) was a small fish known only to occur in Goodenough Spring, Val Verde County, Texas, a tributary of the Rio Grand River. This species was eliminated in the wild when construction of the Amistad Reservoir in 1968 submerged Goodenough Spring under approximately 70 feet of water. The FWS listed the Amistad gambusia as endangered in 1980 at which time it occurred only in captivity (45 *FR* 28721). The two captive populations, held by the University of Texas and the Dexter National Fish Hatchery in New Mexico, died or were eliminated through hybridization and predation. The FWS rule the Amistad gambusia extinct in 1987, and removed it from the endangered species list (52 *FR* 46083).

Dusky Seaside Sparrow

The dusky seaside sparrow subspecies (*Ammodramus maritimus nigrescens*) was a small songbird that existed only on Merritt Island and the upper St. John's River marshes of Brevard County, Florida. Populations of the sparrow declined as its salt marsh habitat was converted to freshwater mosquito-control impoundments, or drained. The use of DDT to control mosquitoes was also suspected as a contributing factor in the species' decline.

Dusky seaside sparrows were first listed as endangered in 1967 under the ESPA (32 *FR* 4001). The last remaining wild birds, all males, were taken into captivity in 1979 and 1980 to begin a captive breeding program. The males were mated with females of a closely related subspecies (Scott's seaside sparrow, *A.m. pennsulae*) to try to preserve their genetic information. The hybrid offspring were not protected under the ESA and the breeding program proved unsuccessful. The last male sparrow died on June 16, 1987, and the hybrid offspring died by the summer of 1989. In 1990, the FWS declared the dusky seaside sparrow extinct and took it off the endangered species list (55 *FR* 51112).

RECOVERED SPECIES

The goal of the ESA is the recovery of a listed species to population levels where protection under the Act is no longer necessary. A species may be classified as recovered if its decline has been halted or reversed, and threats minimized, so that its survival in the wild is likely. According to FWS, there are currently 11 species that have been delisted due to recovery. (See note on Rydberg milk-vetch.)

Brown Pelican

The brow pelican (*Pelecanus occidentalis*) is a large coastal bird with a wingspan of nearly seven feet; it feeds almost exclusively on fishes captured by plunge diving. In the early 1960's, pelican populations suffered dramatic reductions as a result of organochlorine pesticide pollution. The pesticide endrin was thought to kill many pelicans through direct toxic effects, while the pesticide DDT led to eggshell thinning and reproductive failure. The brown pelican was listed under the ESCA as an endangered species throughout its U.S. and foreign ranges in 1970 (35 *FR* 16047 and 35 *FR* 8495). In 1973, the Environmental Protection Agency (EPA) banned the use of DDT in the United States (37 *FR* 13369) and began to sharply curtail the use of endrin. Since that time, pelican populations in the eastern Gulf and Atlantic coastal regions have reached or exceeded their historical breeding levels.

In 1985, the FWS removed the brown pelican from the endangered species list in Alabama, Florida, Georgia, South Carolina, North Carolina, and points northward along the Atlantic coast (50 *FR* 4938). The brown pelican remains endangered throughout the remainder of its range, which includes Mississippi, Louisiana, Texas, California, Mexico, Central and South America, and the West Indies.

Palau Fantail Flycatcher, Palau Ground-Dove, And Palau Owl

The Palau Islands are located east of the Philippines in the South Pacific. They were formerly a U.S. – administered United Nations Trust Territory, and since 1994, have had an independent constitutional government. World War II fighting caused heavy damage to many of the islands, and as a result many populations of native species dramatically declined. The Palau fantail flycatcher (*Rhipidura lepida)*, Palau ground-dove (*Gallicolumba canifrons*), and Palau owl (*Pyrroglaux podargina*) are three native bird species that were virtually eliminated during the war. These species were listed as endangered under the ESCA in 1970 (35 *FR* 8495) based on data from military surveys done shortly after the U.S. invasion of Angaur and Peleiu in 1944.

Since the end of World War II, the fantail flycatcher, ground-dove, and owl have returned to near original abundances and are not faced with any foreseeable threats. None of the species are sought as a game species, and the new constitution of Palau bans the personal possession of firearms, making it illegal to hunt with any type of gun. Based on this evidence, the FWS removed the Palau fantail flycatcher, the Palau ground-dove, and the Palau owl from the endangered species list in 1985 (50 *FR* 37192).

American Alligator

The American alligator (*Alligator mississippiensis)* is a large aquatic reptile that inhabits wetland areas of the southeast Atlantic and Gulf states. It is one of only two species (Chinese alligator and American alligator) of the genus *Alligator.* Overharvesting due to commercial demand for alligator products led to significant population declines during the 1950's and 1960's. In 1967, the FWS listed the alligator as an endangered species under the ESPA. The Lacey Act Amendments of 1969 prohibited interstate commerce in illegally taken reptiles and their parts and products. The heavy penalties added under the ESA of 1973, and the listing in Appendix II of the Convention on International Trade in Endangered Species of Wild Fauna and Flora (CITES) provided further protection against illegal taking. Populations have recovered and are now stable but disjunct, and limited to areas of remaining suitable habitat within their former range.

In 1977, the FWS downlisted the alligator from endangered to threatened in part of its range, including the Florida and certain coastal areas of Georgia, South Carolina, Louisiana, and Texas (42 *FR* 2071). In 1987, the FWS downlisted the American alligator throughout the remainder of its range to "Threatened due to similarity of appearance" (52 *FR* 21059). This classification reflects a complete recovery of the alligator, but is intended to facilitate necessary protections for the American crocodile (*Crocodylus acutus*) in the United States and foreign countries, and other endangered crocodilians in foreign countries, whose products are difficult to distinguish form those of the American alligator. Any proposed harvests under this classification must comply with the FWS's special rule on American alligators (50 CFR §17.42(a)) and existing state statutes and regulations.

Rydberg Milk-Vetch

The Rydberg milk-vetch *(Astragalus periamus)* is a small, flowering plant that occurs in the mountain and plateau region of south central Utah. The FWS listed the milk-vetch as threatened in 1978 based on data shoeing that the plant was known to occur in two locations: Bullion Canyon, Piute County, Utah, and Mt. Dutton, Garfield County, Utah (43 *FR* 17914). Beginning in 1983, the U.S. Forest Service conducted extensive surveys as part of a management plan developed for the Rydberg milk-vetch. The surveys resulted in the discovery of 11 additional populations with estimates of over 300,000 plants. Based on this new information, the FWS delisted the Rydberg milk-vetch in September 1989 (54 *FR* 37941).

The FES has categorized this delisting as a "recovery" in it published list of species removed from the endangered and threatened lists. It should be noted, however, that the information published in the final rule delisting the Rydberg milk-vetch could also be interpreted as an error in the original data.

Gray Whale

Gray whales (*Eschrichtius robustus*) are large marine mammals that can reach lengths of 50 feet. They are bottom feeders whose main diet consists of small crustaceans called amphipods. The eastern North Pacific (California) population spends the summer feeding in the Bering, Chukchi, and Beaufort Seas. After migrating along the western shore of North America, gray whales spend the winter off of the coast of Baja California, where the young are born in shallow lagoons.

Commercial whaling significantly reduced gray whale populations, with estimates of 4,000-5,000 whales remaining by the mid 1800's. In 1947, the International Convention on the Regulation of Whaling banned the commercial harvesting of gray whales, although subsistence harvesting by aboriginal groups was allowed to continue . Since the ban, the eastern population has recovered to nearly the estimated original level, and is now neither in danger of extinction, nor "likely to become endangered within the foreseeable future throughout all or a significant portion of its range." The FWS concurred with the National Marine Fisheries Service's Determination, and delisted the eastern North Pacific (California) population of the gray whale in 1994 (59 *FR* 31094). The western North Pacific (Korea) population remains listed as endangered. Gray whales continue to receive protection under the Marine Mammal Protection Act of 1972 (16 U.S.C. § 1361).

Arctic Peregrine Falcon

The peregrine falcon is a medium-sized brown or blue-gray raptor that preys primarily on birds. Three subspecies of peregrines occur in North America—arctic peregrine falcon *(Falco peregrinus tundrius);* American peregrine falcon *(F. p. anatum)*; and Peale's peregrine falcon *(F. p. pealei)*. Arctic peregrines nest in the tundra regions of Alaska, Canada, and Greenland. They are highly migratory, wintering mostly in Latin America.

Arctic peregrine falcon populations declined in the 1950's and 1960's as a result of contamination with organochlorine pesticides such as DDT. These pesticides can accumulate to lethal levels in the fatty tissues of animals eating contaminated prey. At lower concentrations the principal metabolite of DDT can disrupt eggshell formation, causing eggs to break easily.

Arctic peregrines were protected in 1970 under the ESCA, and subsequently covered in 1973 under the ESA. Populations began to recover when Canada restricted the use of DDT in 1970, followed by an EPA ban on DDT in the United States in 1973 (37 *FR* 13369). The United States restricted the use of other organochlorine pesticides, including aldrin and dieldrin, in 1974. The FWS downlisted the arctic peregrine falcon from endangered to threatened in March 1984 (49 *FR* 10520), and removed it from the list of threatened species in October 1994 (59 *FR* 50796). Arctic peregrines are still protected under the similarity of appearance provision of the ESA listing all *Falco peregrinus* found in the wild in the contiguous 48 states as endangered. Arctic peregrines also continue to be protected under the Migratory Bird Treaty Act (16 U.S.C. §703-712).

Red Kangaroo, Western Gray Kangaroo, Eastern Gray Kangaroo

Kangaroos are large marsupial mammals indigenous to Australia. Marsupial populations in Australia began to decline with European settlement and the expansion of sheep ranching. A dramatic drop in kangaroo populations resulted from the development of a commercial market in kangaroo hides and meat. Citing evidence of excessive commercial utilization, the FWS listed the red kangaroo (*Macropus rufus*), eastern gray kangaroo (*Macropus giganteus*), and western gray kangaroo *(Macropus fuliginosus)* as threatened species in December 1974, and banned the commercial importation of kangaroos, their parts, and products (39 *FR* 44990). The FWS also asserted that Australia's regulatory control of hunting and trade were inadequate.

In April 1981, the FWS lifted the importation ban on the three threatened kangaroos after accepting the management programs of four Australian states. The FWS determining that managed "taking" would not be detrimental to the survival of the species, and removed the red kangaroo, eastern gray kangaroo, and western gray kangaroo from the list of threatened wildlife in 1995 (60 *FR* 12888). A subspecies of eastern gray kangaroo (*M.g. tasmaniensis*) which occurs solely in Tasmania, retains its endangered classification under the ESA.

ORIGINAL DATA FOR CLASSIFICATION IN ERROR

Information collected after a species has been listed as endangered or threatened may show that the data used for listing, or the interpretation of such data, were incomplete, erroneous, or affected by later amendment of the ESA. The FWS determined that it listed eight species based on data that were incomplete or in error. (See note on Rydberg mil-vetch.) These de-listings were the result of: (1) better data, including foreign scientific and commercial information; (2) scientific or taxonomic review on; and (3) discovery of previously unknown populations or habitats. (See http://www.fws.gov/~r9endspp/delisted.pdf for more information.) The FWS listed one species based on data that, as a result of subsequent amendment to the ESA, were determined to no longer be valid criteria for listing.

Mexican Duck

The Mexican duck (once classified as *Anas diazi*) was historically found in Arizona, New Mexico, Texas, and throughout northern Mexico. This species was listed as endangered in 1967 under the ESPA based on evidence of habitat loss and declining populations due to hybridization with the common mallard duck (*A. platyrhynchos*). The Mexican duck was later determined to be a subspecies of *A. platyrhynchos*, and according to the FWS, "the interbreeding of two subspecies of the same species is an expected natural phenomenon. Protection under the definition of 'species' in the Act for one phenotype [an organism's general appearance] in a geographic segment or population of the same species is not permissible." (43 *Fr* 32258). In short, the Mexican duck no longer qualified as sufficiently distinct under the ESA's definition of a species to warrant protection. Moreover, the loss of natural habitat was determined to no longer be a threat, because the species was found to be able to live in newly created agricultural areas. In 1978, the FWS removed the Mexican duck form the endangered species list (43 *Fr* 32258).

Pine Barrens Treefrog

The Pine Barrens treefrog (*Hyla andersonii*) is a small amphibian that occurs in New Jersey, the Carolinas, and Florida. In 1977, the Florida population only was listed as endangered under the ESA based on "the present or threatened destruction, modification, or curtailment of its habitat or range." Surveys at that time showed that there were only seven small breeding sites in Okaloosa County, with less than 500 estimated individuals. Surveys started in 1978 by the Florida Game and Fresh Water Fish Commission found more than 150 additional sites in Okaloosa, Walton, Santa Rosa, and Homes Counties in Florida, and six sites in Escambia and Covington Counties, Alabama. Based on this new evidence, the FWS delisted the Pine Barrens treefrog in 1983 (48 *FR* 52740).

Indian Flap-Shelled Turtle

The Indian flap-shelled turtle (*Lissemys punctata punctata*) is a softshell turtle occurring in southern and central India and Sri Lanka. A closely related turtle, *L. p. andersoni*, occurs in northern India, Pakistan, Nepal, Bangladesh, and Burma. The flap-shelled turtle was placed on Appendix I of CITES in 1975 at the request of Bangladesh. However, *L.p. punctata* was the taxa listed, not *L. p. andersoni*. Under a broad rule placing 159 taxa from Appendix I of CITES on the ESA's List of Endangered and Threatened Wildlife, the FWS listed *L.p. punctata* as endangered in 1976 (41 *FR* 24062). Although *L. p. pimcata* was the subspecies listed by the FWS, its stated range included regions from which *L.p. andersoni*, not *L. p. punctata*, is known to occur. It is unclear which subspecies—*L.p.*

punctata or *L. p. andersoni*, or both—was meant to be included in the CITES and ESA listings.

Subsequent reviews of the literature and available data could find no evidence to support this endangered status. To the contrary, scientists now classify *L.p. punctata* and *L.p. andersoni* as only one subspecies. This subspecies is the most common aquatic turtle in India. Consequently, the FWS removed the Indian flap-shelled turtle from the endangered species list in 1983 (48 *FR* 52740). This action did not affect the turtle's status on Appendix I of CITES.

Bahama Swallowtail Butterfly

The Bahama swallowtail butterfly (*Heraclides (Papilio) andraemon bonhotei*) is a tropical insect whose occurrence n Florida represents the northern limit of its distribution. This dark brown and yellow butterfly is restricted to tropical upland hardwood habitat, now found in the United States primarily in the Florida Keys. It was listed as threatened under the ESA in 1976 (41 *FR* 17736), at which time it was found only in Dade and Monroe Counties, Florida. The Bahama swallowtail was later found to be only a sporadic resident of the United States, and not distinct from the Bahamian population of the same subspecies. Moreover, the 1978 Amendments to the ESA limited protection of the same subspecies. Moreover, the 1978 Amendments to the ESA limited protection at the population level to vertebrates (ESA § 3(15)). As a result of ESA amendment, the FWS took the Bahama swallowtail butterfly off the endangered species list in 1984 (49 *FR* 34501), since it was neither a vertebrate nor a distinct population.

Purple-Spined Hedgehog Cactus

The purple-spined hedgehog cactus (*Echinocereus engelmannii* var. *purpureus*) was first described as a distinct taxonomic group in 1969 from specimens collected near St. George, Utah. It was determined to be very rare and was listed as endangered under the ESA in 1979 (44 *FR* 58866). Subsequent investigations found that the purple-spined hedgehog cactus is simply a dark-colored, short-spined phase that occurs interspersed throughout populations of *E. e. chrysocentrus;* the two types of plants cross-pollinate readily in nature. *Since E. e. chrysocentrus* is common and widely distributed in the Mojave Desert of Arizona, California, Nevada, and Utah, in 1989, the FWS delisted the purple-spined hedgehog cactus (54 *FR* 48749).

Tumamoc Globeberry

The Tumamoc globeberry (*Tumamoca macdougalii*) is a perennial vine in the gourd family with small greenish-yellow flowers and bright red fruits. It occurs from south central Arizona south through southern Sonora, Mexico. The FWS listed the globeberry as endangered under the ESA in 1986 based on the known presence of only 30 isolated populations in Pima County, Arizona, and five populations in Sonora, Mexico (51 *FR* 15906). In 1988 and 1989, the Bureau of Reclamation conducted surveys required by § 7 of the ESA to determine the impact of a Central Arizona Project canal and pipeline on the globeberry. These surveys determined that the species occurred across a more extensive range and was less habitat-specific than previously thought. Finding few threats of extinction in its newly identified habitat, the FWS removed the Tumamoc globeberry from the endangered species list in 1993 (58 *FR* 33562).

Spineless Hedgehog Cactus

Botanist Karl Schuman first described the spineless hedgehog cactus (*Echinocereus triglochidiatus* var. *inermis*) in 1896 from specimens collected in southeast Utah and southwest Colorado. The FWS listed this subspecies as endangered in 1979 under the ESA based on its rare occurrence (44 *FR* 64744). The recovery plan for the spineless hedgehog cactus noted a question of its true taxonomic status, and later studies determined hat it is simply a spineless form of the red-flowered hedgehog cactus (*E. t.* var. *melanacanthus)* that is widely distributed from northern Colorado and Utah to Durango and San Luis Potosi, Mexico. Finding that the spineless hedgehog cactus is "not a discrete and valid taxonomic entity and does not meet the definition of a species (which includes subspecies)," the FWS removed it from the endangered species list in 1993 (58 *FR* 49242).

McKittrick Pennyroyal

The McKittrick pennyroyal (*Hedeoma apiculatum*) is a perennial herb, four to six inches tall, with dense leaves and showy pink flowers. The species is endemic to the Guadalupe Mountains in northwest Texas and southeast New Mexico, where it occurs above 5,400 feet in limestone outcrops. The FWS described this pennyroyal having "limited it as threatened under the ESA in 1982" (47 *FR* 30440). Subsequent surveys found this herb to be more widespread and abundant, and less vulnerable to human disturbance than previously thought. In 1993, the FWS took the McKittrick pennyroyal off the threatened species list (58 *FR* 49245).

Cuneate Bidens

The cuneate bidens (*Bidens cunceata*) is an herb of the thistle family with yellow flowers. It was first described in 1920 from specimens collected on the Hawaiian island of Oahu. The plant was listed as endangered in 1984 based on surveys indication its rare occurrence (49 *Fr* 6099). A recent revision of the Hawaiian members of the *Bidens* genus determined that *B. cuneata* is an outlying population of *B. molokainsis* that is common along the windward cliffs of nearby Molokai island. These new data indicated that cuneate bidens is not a discrete taxonomic entity," resulting in the FWS delisting *B. cuneata* in 1996 (61 *FR* 4372).

DOWNLISTED SPECIES

Species that have stabilized or increased in number may be reclassified from endangered or threatened status. ESA proponents assert that down-listing can be an important part of the recovery process, and a measure of success for the ESA. However, these species are often not counted by opponents as successes for the ESA because they have not met the Act's goal of complete removal from the list. Twenty-two species have been downlisted from endangered to threatened status.

Lahontan Cutthroat Trout, Paiute Cutthroat Trout, Arizona Trout

The Lahontan cutthroat trout (*Oncorhynchus (=Salmo) clarki henshawi*), Paiute cutthroat trout *(O. c. seleniris)*, and Arizona trout *(Oncorhynchus apache)* are western trout species with limited distributions. *O.c. henshawi* occurs in most streams of the Truckee, Carson and Walker River drainages in California and Nevada. *O.c. seleniris* occurs in Silver King Creek and its tributaries in Alpine County, California. *O. apache* occurs in the headwaters of the Salt and Little Colorado Rivers in east central Arizona.

These species were listed as endangered under the ESCA of 1969 due to "destruction, drastic modification, or severe curtailment of their habitat," and hybridization with introduced trout species, especially the brook and rainbow trout. State and federal recovery programs successfully cultured and introduced populations in areas from which they were depleted, and reduced the threat of hybridization by eliminating exotic species. In 1975, the FWS downlisted the Lahontan cutthroat trout, Paiute cutthroat trout, and Arizona trout from endangered to threatened (40 *FR* 29863). A special rule under this downlisting action allows the regulated taking of these species for sport fishing purposes.

American Alligator

See section under "Recovered Species."

Gray Wolf

The gray wolf (*Canis lupus*) was historically found over most of North America, from central Mexico to the Arctic Ocean. Systematic eradication programs, habitat destruction, and over-hunting of prey populations eliminated wolves from most of the contiguous United States by the 1940's. In 1967, the timber wolf subspecies *Canis lupus lycaon*, was listed as endangered under the ESPA of 1966 (32 *FR* 4001). In 1973, the FWS listed the northern Rocky Mountain subspecies, *C.I. irremotus,* and the Texas subspecies, *C.I. monstrabilis,* as endangered under the ESA (38 *FR* 14678). In 1978, the Secretary clarified the legal and taxonomic confusion that arose form these listings by downlisting the Minnesota population of wolves from endangered to threatened, while all other North American gray wolf populations south of Canada remained listed as endangered, without reference to subspecies (43 *FR* 9607).[9]

Greenback Cutthroat Trout

The greenback cutthroat trout *(Oncorhynchus (=Salmo) clarki stomias)* is a fish endemic to the headwaters of the South Platte and Arkansas Rivers in Colorado. Habitat destruction caused by mining, logging, grazing and irrigation projects, in addition to hybridization with introduced trout, drastically reduced populations of the greenback cutthroat. By 1930, this species was believed to be extinct. Later rediscovery allowed state and federal conservation programs to culture and reintroduce populations in it historical range. These programs also

---

[9] For more information, see CRS Report 97-47ENR, *Reintroduction of Wolves.*

eliminated many of the exotic species responsible for hybridization problems.. In 1978, the FWS downlisted the greenback cutthroat trout from endangered to threatened (43 *FR* 16343), recognizing that threats from habitat destruction and hybridization remain. A special rule under this downlisting action allows for the regulated taking of this species for sport fishing purposes.

Red Lechwe

The red lechwe (*Kobus leche*) is a species of African antelope whose historical range included parts of Namibia, Botswana, Angola, Zaire, and Zambia. Unregulated commercial and subsistence hunting, combined with habitat destruction, led to population declines through the first half of the 20th Century. The FWS listed the red lechwe as endangered under the ESCA in 1970 (35 *FR* 8495). Control of hunting and listing on Appendix I of CITES resulted in stable or increasing populations over much of their range. In 1979, the Conference of the parties to CITES changed the listing of the red lechwe from Appendix I to Appendix II, and in 1980, the FWS downlisted the red lechwe from endangered to threatened (45 *FR* 65132). With the Appendix II listing, § 9(c)(2) of the ESA allows "the importation of legally taken sport-hunted trophies."

Leopard

The leopard (*Panthera pardus*) is widely distributed across Africa, China, Japan, Korea, India, Sri Lanka, and Southeast Asia. An uncontrolled commercial fur trade (*e.g.,* the Untied States imported more than 17,000 leopard hides form 1968 to 1969) sharply depleted leopard populations. In 1970, the FWS listed the leopard as endangered under the ESCA (35 *FR* 8495), prohibiting the import of live animals, their parts and products. *P. pardus* was also added to Appendix I of CITES, providing for further control of commercial trade in hides. Subsequent surveys, determined that leopard populations in some areas were recovering, and in 1982, the FWS downlisted the southern African leopard populations from endangered to threatened (47 *FR* 4304). A special rule allows the import of "legally taken sport-hunted leopard trophies." Other populations of leopard remain listed as endangered under the ESA.

Arctic Peregrine Falcon

See section under "Recovered Species."

Utah Prairie Dog

The Utah prairie dog (*Cynomys parvidens*) is a burrowing rodent of the squirrel family that occurs only in southern Utah. Early ranchers believed that the prairie dog competed directly with livestock for food. The ranchers actively sought to eliminate them through habitat alteration and poisoning. In 1973, the FWS listed the Utah prairie dog as endangered under the ESA (38 *FR* 14678), pursuant to the ESCA of 1969. The protections provided by the ESA allowed populations to increase, and in 1984, the FWS downlisted the Utah prairie dog from endangered to threatened (49 *FR* 222330). TO mitigate conflict between ranchers and expanding prairie dog populations, a special rule was included in the downlisting that allows the "taking" of up to 5,000 prairie dogs per year.

Snail Darter

The snail darter (*Percina tanasi*) is a small fish, typically less than 3.5 inches, that occurs in sandbar habitat in six tributaries f the Tennessee River. The FWS listed the snail darter as endangered under the ESA in 1975 (40 *FR* 47506), at which time it was known from only one population at the mouth of the Little Tennessee River. In 1979, federal law exempted the Little Tennessee River Tellico Reservoir Project from the ESA, allowing a dam to be completed that inundated the known population. Before and after dam completion, the FWS introduced the snail darter into other streams in the area with only limited success. Subsequent surveys, however, found populations in six Tennessee River tributaries in Tennessee and Alabama. These discoveries allowed the FWS to downlist the snail darter from endangered to threatened in 1984 (49 *Fr* 27501). This historic conflict between an endangered species and development played a major role in the evolution of the ESA.[10]

---

[10] For more information about the history of this species, which was the centerpiece of arguably the most famous legal battle in the history of the ESA, see CRS Report 90-242ENR, *Endangered Species Act: The Listing and Exemption Process,* Appendix B.

Tinian Monarch

The Tinian monarch (*Monarcha takatsukasae*) is a small brownish song bird that is endemic to the island of Tinian, north of Guam in the Mariana Archipelago. Deforestation, first for sugarcane production, and later as a result of World War II combat activities, caused a severe depletion of the monarch population. The FWS listed the Tinian monarch as endangered in 1970 under the ESCA 35 *FR* 8495) based on pre- and post-war data. The island has since become revegitated with a shrubby legume (*Leucaenz leucoecphala*) in which the monarch has thrived. In 1987, the FWS downlisted the Tinian monarch from endangered to threatened (52 *FR* 10890). The Service noted three threats preventing the complete delisting of the species: 1) potential defoliation of *Leucaena* by introduced plant lice; 2) potential introduction of the predatory brown tree snake (*Boiga irregularis*)[11]; and 3) the species' existence is limited to one small island.

Aleutian Canada Goose

The Aleutian Canada goose *(Branta Canadensis leucopareia),* one of the smallest of 11 subspecies of Canada geese, nests on remote islands off the coast of the Alaska Peninsula and in the Aleutian Archipelago. Most Aleutian geese migrate along the Pacific coast flyway of North America and winter in Oregon and California. Some geese migrate along the western coast of the Pacific and winter in Asia and Japan. Populations of Aleutian geese declined due to arctic fox (*Alopex lagopus)* introductions on their breeding islands, and recreational and subsistence hunting in the Pacific flyway. The FWS added *B. c. leucopareia* to the list of U.S. endangered species under the ESP in 1967 (32 *FR* 4001), and to the list of foreign endangered species under the ESCA in 1970 (35 *FR* 8495). Fox control programs on breeding islands and hunting closures in important wintering areas are primarily responsible for increasing goose populations. In 1990, the FWS downlisted all populations of the Aleutian Canada goose from endangered to threatened (55 *FR* 51106), noting that the species still faces threats from disease, predation, and, especially on the wintering grounds, storms and habitat loss.

---

[11] For more information, see CRS Report 97-507ENR, *Non-Indigenous Species: Government Response to the Brown Tree Snake and Issues for Congress.*

Nile Crocodile

The Nile crocodile (*Crocodylus niloticus*) is a large aquatic reptile that was historically found throughout Africa and as far as north as Syria. Habitat destruction, unregulated commercial trade in hides, and hunting to eliminate threats to humans, livestock, and fisheries led to significant population declines. The crocodile was first listed as endangered under the ESCA in 1970 (35 *FR* 8495), and on Appendix I of CITES in 1975. As countries began to implement management practices, especially ranching for the controlled harvest of hides, crocodile populations stabilized or increased. Zimbabwe's successful management led to a downlisting of their ranched populations in 1987 (52 *FR* 23148), and a downlisting of their wild populations in 1988 (53 *FR* 38451). In 1993, the FWS downlisted all populations of the Nile crocodile from endangered to threatened (58 *FR* 49870). The species has also been moved from Appendix I to Appendix II of CITES in Botswana, Malawi, Mozambique, and Zambia, allowing for regulated commercial trade in crocodile hides from these countries.

Louisiana Pearlshell

The Louisiana pearlshell (*Margaritifera hembeli*) is a freshwater mussel approximately 4" long that was known to exist only in the Bayou Boeuf drainage, Rapides Parish, Louisiana. Due to its limited distribution and threats from destruction of river habitat, the FWS listed this species as endangered under the ESA in 1988 (53 *FR* 3567). Since the listing, *M. hembeli* has been found in the Red River drainage, Grant Parish, Louisiana. Subsequent surveys done under the recovery plan expanded the known range to eight streams of the Red River drainage and 11 streams of the Bayou Boeuf drainage. While the discovery of additional populations removes the immediate threat of extinction, threats remain from population fragmentation by impoundments, collecting, and sedimentation from gravel mining. For these reasons, the FWS downlisted the Louisiana pearlshell from endangered to threatened in 1993 (58 *FR* 49935).

Siler Pincushion Cactus

The Siler pincushion cactus (*Pediocactus sileri*) is a 4-5" spherical or cylindrical cactus with 1" spines and yellow flowers. It is found primarily on gypsum soils at altitudes between 2,800 and 5,400 feet in southwest Utah and northwest Arizona. The FWS listed this species as endangered under the ESA in

1979 (44 *FR* 61786) based on evidence that its small populations with limited habitat were threatened by gypsum mining, off-road vehicle use, road construction, collection, livestock, and development of the Warner Valley Power Plant. Under the Siler Pincushion Cactus Recovery Plan, the FWS closed certain areas to off-road vehicles, fenced off areas of high cactus density, and surveyed potential habitat. As cactus was no longer in danger of extinction, and in 1993, downlisted it from endangered to threatened (58 *FR* 68476).

Small Whorled Pogonia

The small whorled pogonia (*Isotria medeoloides*) is a perennial orchid that inhabits young and maturing stands of mixed-deciduous or mixed-deciduous/coniferous forests. The species was widely distributed from southern Maine and New Hampshire, through the Atlantic seaboard states, to southern Tennessee and northern Georgia. The FS listed *I. medeoloides* as endangered under the ESA in 1983 (47 *FR* 39827) when they estimated less than 500 individuals remained in 17 populations. Since listing, the FWS has identified three primary population centers: 1) the Appalachian foothills of New England; 2) the Blue Ridge mountains where Tennessee, North and South Carolina, and Georgia share borders; and 3) coastal plain and piedmont countries of Virginia. Management actions at these and other sites have provided adequate protection and allowed populations to stabilize or increase to meet recovery plan objectives. Thus, the FWS downlisted the small whorled pogonia from endangered to threatened in 1994 (59 *FR* 50852).

Virginia Round-Leaf Birch

The Virginia round-leaf birch *(Betula uber)* is a species from southwestern Virginia with smooth, dark-brown or black bark that can reach heights of 45 feet. Botanists assumed this species to be extinct when no specimens could be found from 1950 to 1975. In 1975, 41 trees were found along specimens could be found from 1950 to 1975. In 1975, 41 trees were found along Cressy Creek, Smyth County, Virginia. Due to its limited population, the FWS listed *B. uber* as endangered under the ESA in 1978 (43 *FR* 17910). Although this natural population declined from vandalism and transplantation in the late 1970's, a FWS recovery plan established additional populations through propagation management with the help of the U.S. National Arboretum, the Virginia Agricultural Experimental Station, and others. Populations have met recovery plan goals, and in 1994, the FWS downlisted the Virginia round-leaf birch from endangered to threatened (59 *FR* 59173).

Bald Eagle

The bald eagle (*Haliaeetus leucocephalus*) is typically associated with estuaries, large lakes, major rivers, and seacoast habitats. Its historical range included most of North America from central Alaska and Canada to northern Mexico. Beginning in the mid to late 1800's a decline in eagle populations was attributed to a drop in waterfowl and shorebird prey populations, direct killing, and habitat destruction. The Bald Eagle Protection Act of 1940 (16 U.S.C. 668) prohibited direct killing in most of the eagle's range except Alaska, where the state paid a bounty for killing eagles to protect the salmon fishery. In 1952, the exemption allowing Alaska's bounty was revoked.

Following World War II, the widespread use of the organochlorine pesticide DDT caused significant reproductive failure, leading to another sharp decline in eagle populations. DDE, the primary breakdown product of DDT, caused eggshells to be thin and to break easily. The FWS listed bald eagle populations south of the 40th parallel as endangered under the ESPA in 1967 (32 *FR* 4001). In 1978, he FWS listed all remaining birds in the lower 48 states as endangered under the ESA, with the exception of populations in Michigan, Minnesota, Wisconsin, Oregon, and Washington, where eagles were listed as threatened (43 *FR* 6233). The EPA banned the use of DDT in the United States in 1973 (37 *FR* 13369). Bald eagle recovery plans were developed in each of five established recovery regions. With annual spending exceeding $1 million during the period 1985-1995, eagle populations have increased across most of the United States. FWS data for 1995 estimate 4,712 breeding pairs in the lower 48 states, up from a low of 417 pairs in 1963. In 1995, the FWS downlisted the bald eagle from endangered to threatened in all of the lower 48 states (60 *FR* 36000).

McFarlane's Four-O'clock

MacFarlane's four-o'clock (*Mirabilis macfarlanei*) is a perennial plant with hemispherical clumps 24-47" in diameter, and large, funnel-shaped magenta flowers. The species was described in 1936 from a population found along Snake Rive, Oregon. From 1947 to the mid-1970's *M. macfarlanei* was not found and was thought to be extinct. In 1977, two populations were located containing approximately 27 individual plants. The FWS listed the four-o'clock as endangered under the ESA in 1979 based on this limited distribution (44 *FR* 61912). Extensive surveys conducted as part of the species' 1985 recovery plan located over 7,000 plants in three disjunct areas: the Snake River unit, Idaho County, Idaho, and Wallowa County, Oregon; the Salmon River unit, Idaho County, Idaho; and the Imnaha River unit, Wallowa County, Oregon. With reclassification objectives of the recovery plan met, the FWS downlisted MacFarlane's four-o'clock form endangered to threatened in 1996 (61 *Fr* 10693), but noted that continued threats from habitat loss warrant continued protection as a threatened species.

Maguire Daisy

The Maguire daisy (*Erigeron maguirei)* is a perennial herb both and white and orange flowers that is endemic to sandstone canyons and mesas of San Rafael Swell, Emery County, Utah, and Capitol Reef, Wayne County, Utah. In 1985, the FWS listed *E. m.* var. *maguirei* as an endangered species under the ESA due to its limited distribution (50 *FR* 36090). Later studies determined that populations formerly recognized as *E. m. var. maguirei* and *E. m.* var. *harrisonii* "do not merit recognition as separate varieties." By considering these two former varieties as a dingle unit of *E. maguirei*, the FS found there to be more individuals than previously believed. In 1996, the FWS downlisted the Maguire daisy from endangered to threatened (61 *FR* 31054), noting that the small, reproductively isolated populations continue to face threats from mineral development, recreation activities, livestock trampling, and loss of genetic variability.

Australian Saltwater Crocodile

The saltwater crocodile (*Crocodylus porosus)* is a large aquatic reptile distributed across southwest India, Southeast Asia, the Pacific Islands, and the northern coast of Australia. Due to habitat loss, unregulated hunting, and poaching for a commercial trade in hides, all populations of the saltwater crocodile, except for Papua New Guinea's (where the species was somewhat more healthy), were moved from Appendix II to Appendix I of CITES in 1979. In the same year, the FWS listed all populations outside Papua New Guinea as endangered under the ESA (44 *FR* 75074). In 1985, Australia's saltwater crocodiles were returned from Appendix I to Appendix II of CITES due to their successful management of wild and ranched populations. The Appendix II listing of CITES allows for the export of ranch-produced hides. In 1996, the FWS downlisted the Australian population of saltwater crocodile from endangered to threatened, with a special rule that allows the import of ranched crocodiles and their products (61 *FR* 32356). The FWS has proposed a classification of Papua New Guinea's population of crocodile as threatened due to similarity of appearance (59 *FR* 18652).

APPENDIX: REGULATIONS FOR AMENDING LISTS OF ENDANGERED AND THREATENED WILDLIFE AND PLANTS

50 CFR § 424.11 Factors for Listing, Delisting, or Reclassifying Species

(a) Any species or taxonomic group of species (*e.g.*, genus, subgenus) as defined in § 424.02(k) is eligible for listing under the Act. A taxon of higher rank than species may be listed only if all included species are individually found to be endangered or threatened. In determining whether a particular taxon or population is a species for the purposes of the Act, the Secretary shall rely on standard taxonomic distinctions and the biological expertise of the Department and the scientific community concerning the relevant taxonomic group.

(b) The Secretary shall make any determination required by paragraphs (c) and (d) of this section *solely* on he basis of the best available scientific and commercial information regarding a species' status, without reference to possible economic or other impacts of such determination.

(c) A species shall be listed or reclassified if the Secretary determines, on the basis of the best scientific and commercial data available after conducting a review o the species' status, that the species is endangered or threatened because of any one or a combination of the following factors:

    (1) The present or threatened destruction, modification, or curtailment of its habitat or range;

    (2) Over-utilization for commercial, recreational, scientific, or educational purposes;

    (3) Disease or predation;

    (4) The inadequacy of existing regulatory mechanisms; or

    (5) Other natural or manmade factors affecting its continued existence

(d) The factors considered in delisting a species are those in paragraph (c) this section as they relate to the definitions of endangered or threatened species. Such removal must be supported by the best scientific and commercial data available to the Secretary after conducting a review of the status of the species. A species may be delisted only if such data substantiate that it is neither endangered nor threatened for one or more of the following reasons:

    (1) *Extinction.* Unless all individuals of the listed species had been previously identified and located, and were later found to be extirpated from their previous range, a sufficient period of time must be allowed before delisitng to indicate clearly that the species is extinct.

    (2) *Recovery.* The principal goal of the U.S. Fish and Wildlife Service and the National Marine Fisheries Service is to return listed species to a point at which protection under the Act is no longer required. A species may be delisted on the basis of recovery only if the best scientific and commercial data available indicate that it is no longer endangered or threatened.

    (3) *Original data for classification in error.* Subsequent investigations may show that the best scientific and commercial data available when the species was listed, or the interpretation of such data, were in error.

(e) The fact that a species of fish, wildlife, or plant is protected by the Convention on International Trade in Endangered Species of Wild Fauna and Flora (see part 23 of this title 50) or a similar international agreement on such species, or has been identified as requiring protection from unrestricted commerce by any foreign nation, or to be in danger of extinction or likely to become so within the foreseeable future by any State agency or by any agency of a foreign nation that is responsible for the conservation of fish, wildlife, or plants, may constitute evidence that the species is endangered or threatened. The weight given such evidence will vary depending on the international agreement in question, the criteria pursuant to which the species is eligible for protection under such authorities, and the degree of protection afforded the species. The Secretary shall give consideration to any species protected under such an international agreement, or by any State or foreign nation, to determine whether the species is endangered or threatened.

(f) The Secretary shall take into account, in making determination under paragraph (c) or (d) of this section, those efforts, if any, being made by any State or foreign nation, or any political subdivision of a State or foreign nation, to protect such species, whether by predator control, protection of habitat and food supply, or other conservation practices, within any area under its jurisdiction, or on the high seas.

Chapter 6

HABITAT MODIFICATION AND THE ENDANGERED SPECIES ACT: THE *SWEET HOME* DECISION

Pamela Baldwin

On June 29, 1995, the Supreme Court in a 6-3 decision in *Babbitt v. Sweet Home Chapter of Communities for a Great Oregon* upheld the regulation of the Fish and Wildlife Service defining "harm" for purposes of the "take" prohibitions of the Endangered Species Act.[1] The regulation includes significant habitat modification within the meaning of "harm." The *Sweet Home* decision resolves a difference between the 9th Circuit, which had upheld the regulation,[2] and the D.C. Circuit, which had struck it down.[3]

The Endangered Species Act (ESA) prohibits the "take" of endangered species and threatened species that are by regulation given similar protection. "Take" is defined in the Act as "to harass, harm, pursue, hunt, shoot, wound, kill, trap, capture, or collect, or to attempt to engage in any such conduct."[4] There is no additional statutory elaboration on the meaning of take. Beginning in 1975, the

---

[1] U.S. No. 94-859; 1995 LEXIS 4463.

[2] Pailila v. Hawaii Department of Land and Natural Resources, 639 F. 2d 495 (9th Cir. 1981) (Palila I); 852 F. 2d 1106 (9th Cir. 1988) (Palila II).

[3] The D.C. Circuit initially upheld the regulation, but later reversed: Sweet Home Chapter of Communities for a Great Oregon v. Babbitt, 1 F. 3d 1 (D.C. Cir. 1993); 17 F. 3d 1463 (D.C. Cir. 1994).

[4] 16 U.S.C. §1532(19)

Secretary of Interior, through the Director of the Fish and Wildlife Service, promulgated regulations that, among other things, defined "harm":

> *Harm* in the definition of 'take' in the Act means an act that actually kills or injures wildlife. Such act may include significant habitat modification or degradation where it actually kills or injures wildlife by significantly impairing essential behavioral patterns, including breeding, feeding, or sheltering.[5]

Plaintiffs in the case were landowners, companies, families affected by listings, and organizations that represented them. The case was brought as a declaratory judgment action challenging the validity of the regulation *on its face*, *rather than as applied* in any particular instance, and focusing particularly on the inclusion of habitat modification in the regulatory definition.

The Court found that the text of the ESA supports the regulation in three ways. First, "harm" must have some meaning different from the other verbs in the series and hence must mean something beyond physical force directed at a listed creature. The common meaning of the term is broad and in the context of the ESA it would naturally encompass habitat modification that injures or kills members of an endangered species. Second, the purpose of the ESA are broad, including the conservation of ecosystems on which endangered and threatened species depend. Third, in 1982 Congress amended the ESA, presumably with an awareness of the then-current regulation and the first *Palila* case and not only did not correct the regulation, but added the §10 authorization for "incidental take permits" allowing the taking of listed species in certain circumstances as part of otherwise lawful activities the purpose of which was not taking listed species, but could foreseeably result in take.

On these points, the majority disagreed with the analysis of the D.C. Circuit and with the dissenters, and further noted that neither the §5 authority to acquire habitat lands nor §7 provisions on federal compliance precluded the validity of the regulation. And, given the posture of the case, the regulation should be upheld in light of the fact that it was a reasonable interpretation of the statute by the Secretary, to whom Congress had delegated broad discretion and therefore was entitled to some degree of deference. The majority also felt the legislative history of the statute supported the interpretations stated in the regulation; the dissent disagreed on this point as well.

Justice O'Connor, writing in concurrence, emphasized that the challenge before the Court was a facial challenge to the regulation and that the limitation in

---

[5] 50 C.F.R. §17.3. This regulation has been in place since 1975, but was amended in 1981 to emphasize that actual death or injury of a protected animal is necessary for a violation.

the regulation to significant habitat modification that causes actual death or injury to identifiable protected animals (including preventing particular individuals from breeding) and the limitations resulting from the application of ordinary principles or proximate causation, which introduce notions of foreseeability, would result in reasonable applications. She also questioned the applicability of the regulation in the *Palila II* case because the actions of the state might not have proximately caused actual injury or death to living birds.

Justice Scalia, joined in dissent by Justices Rehnquist and Thomas, asserted that the effects of the regulation on private property were not supported by the statute. First, the regulation prohibits *any* habitat modification that kills or injures, regardless of whether that result is intended or foreseeable and no matter how long the chain of causality is between the modification and injury. Second, the regulation includes omission as well as commission of actions. Third, because the regulation includes impairment of breeding, the regulation encompasses injury inflicted not only on individual animals, but upon populations of species. Justice Scalia could find no basis for these elements either in the Act or in the traditional meaning of "take."

Chapter 7

THE ENDANGERED SPECIES ACT AND CLAIMS OF PROPERTY RIGHTS "TAKINGS": A CASE LAW SUMMARY

Robert Meltz

ABSTRACT

The federal Endangered Species Act (ESA) has long been one of the major flash points in the "property rights" debate. This report compiles the court decisions in cases challenging ESA-based measures as a "taking" of property under the Fifth Amendment. The cases address four kinds of ESA measures: (1) prohibitions on land uses that might adversely affect species listed as endangered or threatened; (2) reductions in water delivery to preserve in stream flows needed by listed fish; (3) limits on the defensive measures a property owner may take to protect his/her property from listed animals, and (4) limits on commercial dealings in members of species acquired prior to listing as endangered or threatened. To date, only one of these decisions has found a taking, and that decision is still subject to appeal.

The federal Endangered Species Act (ESA),[1] along with its state counterparts, has long been one of the major flash points in the "property rights" debate. In the ESA context, the debate has at least two components. First, to what extent must or should implementation of the ESA include restrictions on the use of privately owned property? And second, given that such restrictions are imposed, to what extent does the Constitution, specifically the Takings Clause of the Fifth

---

[1] 16 U.S.C. §§ 1531-1544.

Amendment,[2] demand that compensation be paid to the property owner? This second question is or focus here.

Much scholarly writing exists on the question of what ESA impacts on the property owner must, constitutionally, be compensated as "takings."[3] A comprehensive analytic review was provided in 1993 on how the takings issue has played out under the ESA and other federal and state wildlife protections.[4] This new report simply compiles the ESA takings court decisions to date, with brief comment. Renewed congressional interest ahs been prompted by the recent, highly significant decision of the U.S. Court of Federal Claims in *Tulare Lake Basin Water Storage District v. United States*,[5] holding that federal water use restrictions imposed under the ESA constituted a taking. This is the first time that any ESA-mandated measure has been held by a court to be a taking.

The ESA takings decisions address court types of impacts that the Act has had on private property owners:

1. Prohibitions on Land Uses that Might Adversely Affect Listed Species

Good v. United States, 189 F. 3d 1355 (fed. Cir. 1999), *cert. Denied*, 120 S. Ct. 1554 (2000*)*

In 1973, plaintiff bought a 40-acre, mostly-wetlands tract in the Florida Keys, and in 1980 began efforts to secure the federal, state, and local permits needed to construct a residential subdivision there. Though the Corps of Engineers issued wetlands permits twice, construction did not begin because of state and local permitting, and ESA, problems. Both of the Corps permits expired. Plaintiff's final application to the Corps, at issue here, was denied in 1994 on the ground that the proposed project would endangered the continued existence of the Lower Keys marsh rabbit and the silver rice rat, listed as endangered in 1990 and 1991 respectively.

---

[2] The Takings Clause of the Fifth Amendment states: [N]or shall private property be taken for public use, without just compensation."

[3] *See e.g.*, Glenn P. Sugameli, *The ESA and Takings of Private Property*, in THE ENDANGERED SPECIES ACT HANDBOOK (American Bar Ass'n, forthcoming 2001) (pre-publication draft available from author at sugameli@nwf.org); Comment, *Denial of Permission to "Take" an Endangered Species Will Amount to a "Taking" Under the Fifth Amendment in Limited Situations*, 21 U. ARK. LITTLE ROCK L. REV. 519 (1999); Blaine I. Green, *The Endangered Species Act and Fifth Amendment Takings: Constitutional Limits of Species Protection*, 15 YALE J. ON REG. 329 (1998).

[4] Robert Meltz, *The Endangered Species Act and Private Property: A Legal Primer*, CRS Report No. 93-346 A (March 7, 1993).

[5] *See* discussion of decision on page 4.

Held, there was no taking of plaintiff's tract. Plaintiff claims that the effect of the Corps' action was to *completely* eliminate any economic use of his property-known in taking law as a *Lucas* "total taking."[6] Even with a total taking claim, however, a property owner must show that his reasonable investment-backed expectations were frustrated. Plaintiff here could not have had a reasonable investment-backed expectation when he bought the property in 1973 that he would obtain approval to fill the wetland. By 1973, the Corps had denied dredge-and-fill permits solely on environmental grounds. And at the time he bought the property, plaintiff acknowledged in the sales contract the difficulty of time he bought the property, plaintiff acknowledged in the sales contract the difficulty of obtaining the necessary federal (and state) permits. Finally, plaintiff waited seven years after purchasing the property before applying for the necessary permits, as wetlands protection and endangered species laws became increasingly stringent. While these developments do not bar the taking claim, they reduce plaintiff's ability to claim surprise when the permit application was denied.

Comment: The *Good* decision takes a broad view of the "notice rule" –the case law doctrine that no regulatory taking occurs when the government restricts a property use under a law existing when the property was acquired, or under a law whose adoption after the property was acquired could have been foreseen. Mr. Good bought his wetlands before the ESA was enacted in its modern form, and 17-18 years before the species that triggered the permit denial were listed.

The holding of the *Good* panel as to the notice rule (that the rule applies even to total taking claims) was contravened later by an opposite holding of another Federal Circuit panel. *Palm Beach Isles Assocs. V. United States*, 208 F. 3d 1374, 1379 n.3 (Fed. Cir.), *and on petition for rehearing*, 231 F. 3d 1354 (Fed. Cir. 2000).

A case pending before the U.S. Supreme Court may yield a decision addressing some of these notice rule issues. *Palazzolo v. Rhode Island*, 746 A.2d 707 (R.I.), *cert. Granted*, 69 U.S.L.W. 3002 (Oct. 10, 2000) (No. 99-2047).

Four Points Utility Joint Venture v. United States, 40 Env't Rep. Cas. (BNA) 1509 (W.D. Tex. 1994).

Plaintiffs-developers allege that to protect endangered and threatened species in the area, the United States "by coercion and by threatening criminal penalties" attempted to prevent the building of a multi-use development in Austin, Texas. Plaintiffs believe that no "take" of a protected species under the ESA will occur, and therefore did not apply for an "incidental take permit."[7]

---

[6] *See* Lucas v. South Carolina Coastal Council, 505 U.S. 1003 (1992).

[7] The word "take" is used by the ESA in a manner entirely different from its use in the Fifth Amendment. In the ESA, "take" means to "harass, harm, pursue, hunt, shoot, would, kill, trap,

Held, plaintiffs must apply for an incidental take permit before the court may properly consider the merits of plaintiffs' claims. Until the Fish and Wildlife Service (FWS) rules on such an application, the Fifth Amendment taking claim is not ripe. Parenthetically, the Service has not taken any definitive action to block the development.

> *Comment*: Observers have noted that the number of takings claims based on ESA restrictions is rather small given the decibel level of the property rights debate that the statute has long inspired. Some have suggested that one reasons for the case law scarcity might be the difficulty in ripening a takings claim under the ESA.[8]

Taylor v. United States, No. 99-131 L (fed. Cl. Order filed Aug. 18, 1999).

Plaintiff submitted an application for an incidental take permit under the ESA. The FWS, however, refused to process it until plaintiff agreed to the mitigation measures that the agency proposed. At the same time, the FWS refused to deny the application.

Held, the taking claim is ripe notwithstanding the absence of a formal denial of plaintiff's application. The FWS has demanded that plaintiff do everything it wants *before* accepting the application. Plaintiff declined, believing the demand mitigation measures to be overly restrictive. In such an instance, the government has made clear the bare minimum that it will accept, so the final, definitive government position required for a ripe taking claim exists despite the lack of a formal ruling on a permit application.

2. Reductions in Water Delivery in Order to Preserve Instream Flows Needed by Listed Species

Tulare Lake Basin Water Storage District v. United States, No. 98-101 L (Fed Cl. April 30, 2001)

In 1992-1994, the federal government reduced the amount of water pumped from the Sacramento-San Joaquin Delta in California, in order to ensure river flow sufficient to protect two species of fish protected under the ESA. The result

---

capture, or collect" an animal. ESA §3(19). The Act makes it unlawful for any person to "take" a listed endangered animal, ESA §9(a)(1)(B)-(C), but provides for certain exceptions, as when the person first obtains an "incidental take permit" under ESA § 10(a)(1)(B). By contrast, "take" in the Fifth Amendment refers to government actions that so severely impinge on private property rights as to "take" the property.

[8] James Rosen, *Private Property and the Endangered Species Act: Has the Doctrine of Ripeness Stymied Legitimate Takings Claims?,* 6 HASTINGS W. –N.W> J. ENV'L L. & POL'Y (1999).

of the reduced pumping was to cut the amount of water made available to the California State Water Project, which, in turn, reduced the amount of water delivered to two of the plaintiffs, the Tulare Lake Basin WSD and the Kern County Water Agency. Other plaintiffs in the case received less water by virtue of being subcontractors to Tulare and Kern.

Held, there was a taking of plaintiffs' right to use the water, in the amount of the reduction. Plaintiffs' contracts conferred a right to the exclusive use of prescribed quantities of water. Thus, a mere restriction on use (as to the water not delivered) completely eviscerates the right, and constitutes a physical taking. The government has essentially substituted itself as the beneficiary of the contract right and totally displaced the contract holder. And the terms of plaintiffs' contracts held harmless for reduced water delivery only the state, not the federal government. Finally, background principles of state law (pubic trust doctrine, doctrine of reasonable use, and nuisance law do not limit plaintiffs' right to use the water, since that right was defined by their contracts and the state's water allocations scheme. The state may change the contracts and its water allocation scheme to reflect these state-law background principles, but critically here, it chose not to do so in the 992-1994 period.

> *Comment:* This decision may be appealed by the United States, thus its permanence is unclear. If not appealed, or if affirmed on appeal, the question will be to what extent it generalizes to users of water from other federal projects.

3. Limits on the Defensive Measures a Property Owner May Take to Protect His/Her Property from Harm by Animals of a Listed Species

Christy v. Hodeel, 857 F.2d 1324 (9th Cir. 1988). *Cert. Denied,* 490 U.S. 1114 (1989)

In 1982, grizzly bears began attacking Christy's herd of sheep, which he grazed on leased land in Montana. By July 9, the bear had killed about 20 sheep. That evening, Christy shot and killed a grizzly bear moving toward his herd. FWS efforts to catch the bears were unsuccessful, with the result that Christy lost a total of 84 sheep to the bears by the time he removed his sheep from the leased land. The Department of the Interior assessed a $3,000 civil penalty against Christy for killing the bear, grizzlies being a listed threatened species under the ESA. A Department administrative law judge reduced the fine to $2,500.

Held, there was no taking of the sheep. Undoubtedly, the bears had physically taken them, but such takings cannot be attributed to the federal government.

Caselaw generally rejects the proposition that the government is answerable for the conduct of protected wildlife – prior to their being reduced to possession by capture, which did not occur here. Neither is there a regulatory taking; the losses sustained by plaintiffs are the incidental result of reasonable regulation n the public interest.

> *Comment. Christy* remains the leading case for the proposition that government limits on the defensive measures available to property owners against marauding animals do not constitute takings. In lone dissent from the denial of certiorari, Justice White asked whether "a Government edict barring one from resisting the loss of one's property is the constitutional equivalent of an edict taking such property in the first place." 490 U.S. at 1115-1116.

4. Limits on Commercial Dealings in Species Acquired Prior to Listing

United States v. Kepler, 531 F. 2d 796 (6th Cir. 1976)

As of the effective date of the ESA in 1973, Kepler allegedly held several animals for lawful purposes under the ESA. Thereafter, he transported tow of them, a cougar and a leopard, from Florid to the "Dogpatch Zoo" in Kentucky – where he was arrested and the animals seized by Department of the Interior agents. He was later convicted of violating the ESA ban against interstate transport of endangered species in the course of a commercial activity.[9]

Held, there is no taking by virtue of plaintiff's animals being seized and his being subject to criminal prosecution for the attempted sale of them. The ESA does not prevent *all* sales of endangered wildlife, only those in interstate or foreign commerce. The Act does not reach intrastate sales, and presumably Kepler could have sold the animals in Florida. In addition ESA section 10 allows the interstate transport or sale of endangered animals if the Secretary of the Interior approves it for scientific purposes. These remaining uses of the animals deflect the taking claim.

United States v Hill, 896 F. Supp. 1057 (D. Colo. 1995).

A criminal indictment charged Hill with the sale of parts of various endangered species (black rhinoceros, tiger, clouded leopard, and snow leopard), in violation of the ESA.

Held, there was no taking of Hill's property interest in these animal parts. Hill has not been denied all economic use of his property, since personal property may

---

[9] ESA §9(a)(10(E).

have value or generate income in ways other than by sale. Further, the ESA permits one to sell endangered and threatened species if one obtains a permit under section 10 of the Act. Finally, at the time Hill acquired the animal parts in the early 980s. they were already subject to the ESA proscriptions at issue here. Therefore, he obtained no property right to sell the animals and so lost no right for which he can claim compensation.

Comment. The *Hill* decision relies heavily on *Andrus v. Allard,* 4444 U.S. 51 (1979), the only U.S. Supreme Court takings decision that directly deals with wildlife protection. *Andrus* addressed the Eagle Protection Act and Migratory Bird Treaty Act, which ban commercial transactions in bird parts even if they were lawfully acquired prior to the ban. The Court found no taking, explaining that while the ban foreclosed the most profitable use of the bird parts (sale), other uses, including possession, transport, donation, or exhibition for an admissions charge, remained to the plaintiffs.

Chapter 8

THE ROLE OF DESIGNATION OF CRITICAL HABITAT UNDER THE ENDANGERED SPECIES ACT

Pamela Baldwin

ABSTRACT

On June 14th, 1999, the Fish and Wildlife Service (FWS) called for public comment on its current procedures for designating critical habitat. In addition, a proposal is before the Senate (S. 1100) to move the time at which critical habitat must be designated for a species under the Endangered Species Act (ESA) from being (basically concurrent with the listing of the species to the time a recovery plan is finalized for that species. This report is written as background for considering the current legislative proposal and the FWS notice and may be updated as circumstances warrant.

INTRODUCTION

On June 14th, 1999, the Fish and Wildlife Service (FWS) in the Department of the Interior published a notice calling for public comment on the current system for designation of critical habitat in order to revise its administrative procedures. The Agency made certain assertions regarding the role of critical habitat designation under the Endangered Species Act (ESA).[1] In addition, a proposal currently is before the Senate (S. 1100) to move the time at which critical habitat must be designated for a species listed under the ESA from being (basically) concurrent with the listing of the species to the time a recovery plan is finalized for that species. This report[2] is written as background for considering both the current legislative proposal and the FWS notice.[3]

There is general agreement that the protection of the habitat upon which a dwindling species depends is essential to its survival and recovery, but how to go about protecting habitat is a complicated question that the ESA does not address fully. Treatment of habitat issues has been evolving over the years of amendments to the ESA. One of the purposes of the ES is to "provide a means whereby the ecosystems upon which endangered species and threatened species depend may be conserved,"[4] and the Act protects habitat in many ways, including: under one aspect of the definition of prohibited "take;" and through purchase of lands, cooperative programs with states, consultation on federal actions or actions with a federal nexus, and issuance of incidental take permits based, in part, on habitat protection. The Act also authorizes the designation of "critical habitat." Designation serves several important express purposes and also informs other aspects of habitat protection under the ACT. Designation of critical habitat may have fewer consequences than many members of the public seem to believe, but may have more consequences than the FWS asserts.

Critical habitat is required to be designated at the time a species is listed under the ESA as endangered or threatened unless designation would not be prudent or the critical habitat is not determinable.[5] "Critical habitat" is defined as areas essential for the "conservation" of the species in question. "Conservation" is defined as using all means necessary to bring a species to the point it no longer needs the protection of the Act—i.e. recovery.[6] All federal agencies are to use their authorities to conserve species and the ecosystems upon which they depend.[7] Habitat currently occupied by a listed species, "may require special management considerations or protection.: This language might have supported direct regulation of lands within critical habitat, but has not been so interpreted.

---

[1] Act of December 28, 1973, Pub. L. 93-205, 87 Stat. 884, as amended, codified at 16 U.S.C. §§ 1531 *et seq.*
[2] This report does not address the conservation of plant species listed as threatened or endangered.
[3] 64 Fed. Reg. 31871 (June 14, 1999).
[4] 16 U.S.C. § 1531(b).
[5] 16 U.S.C. § 1533(b0(6)(C).
[6] 16 U.S.C. § 1532(3)
[7] 16 U.S.C. § 1531(b) and (c).

"Unoccupied" habitat is additional suitable area necessary for the conservation of the species.[8]

The appropriate Secretary[9] must designate critical habitat on the basis of the best scientific data available and after taking into consideration the economic impact, and any other relevant impact, of designating a particular area as critical habitat. He Secretary may exclude an area from designation if the Secretary determines that the benefits of such exclusion outweigh the benefits of specifying an area as part of critical habitat, unless he determines, based on the nest scientific and commercial data available, that the failure to designate the area will result in the extinction of the species concerned.[10] Actions of the Secretary in designating critical habitat are judicially reviewable.[11]

EXPRESS ROLES OF CRITICAL HABITAT

The designation of critical habitat plays several express and direct roles under the ESA.

1. Designation Forces Consideration of Economic and Other Effects

The process of designation of critical habitat requires the Secretary to consider what habitat is essential for conservation of the species and also the economic and other effects of including certain habitat areas. Designation ensures that the needs of the species will be considered at the same time as the consequences of those needs. Alternatives in terms of areas to be included and management actions that might be taken or recommended necessarily are considered.

2. The Designation Process Provides Guidance for Landowners

Similarly, the process of designating critical habitat will result in publication of guidance to landowners through consideration of the need for "special management and protection" of areas within the designated habitat. There appear

---

[8] 16 U.S.C. § 1532(5)(A). The distinction between occupied and unoccupied habitat intended by Congress is not clear.

[9] Responsibility for terrestrial and freshwater species rests with the Secretary if the Interior, while responsibility for marine and anadromous fish rests with the Secretary of Commerce.

[10] 16 U.S.C. § 1533(b). In practice, few areas have been excluded.

to be public misperceptions that designation results in binding restrictions on private lands. In fact, designation forces consideration of all aspects of the habitat needs of a species and generates guidance to landowners, but has not been interpreted as authorizing direct regulation. Guidance typically addresses activities *not* likely to be viewed as prohibited "takes" and activities regarding which a landowner may wish to seek additional guidance to avoid takes.

3. Designation Requires "Consultation" on Federal Actions

Section 7 of the ESA (16 U.S.C. § 1536) requires each federal agency to insure that any action authorized, funded, or carried out by the agency is not likely to jeopardize the continued existence of a listed species or *"result in the destruction or adverse modification of..."* critical habitat. (Emphasis added.) If an action is likely to jeopardize or result in adverse modification of critical habitat, the agency must consult with the FWS (or the National Marine Fisheries Service of the Secretary of Commerce is the responsible Secretary). Note that under the statutory language consultation is triggered by either jeopardy or adverse modification of critical habitat. The consultation process applies to all actions by federal agencies and to all actions with a federal nexus through an approval, permit, or funding, if there is reason to believe that a listed species may be present in the project area and is likely to be affected by project activities. Consultation entails study of the likely effects of project actions, a statement by the Secretary on whether jeopardy or adverse modification is found and suggestions for reasonable and prudent alternatives to the harmful aspects of the proposed project in order to avoid jeopardy or adverse modification of critical habitat. All but a few projects have proceeded under an "incidental take" permit that allows limited takes of the listed species as an incidental part of the implementation of the project in question.

4. Designation Provides an Opportunity for Judicial Review

Designation of critical habitat is a statutory duty and the actions and non-actions of the FWS in this regard can be judicially reviewed.[12] The adequacy of agency consideration of the habitat needs of the species, the economic and other

---

[11] 16 U.S.C. § 1533(g)(1)(C).

[12] *Id.*

impacts of designation, and possible alternatives for critical habitat configuration may reviewed.

INDIRECT EFFECTS OF CRITICAL HABITAT DESIGNATION

The designation of critical habitat also plays several indirect roles in the conservation of species. While any agency studies of the general habitat is a required duty that must include the elements discussed above and is specifically reviewable by the courts. It also is currently required to precede other actions that logically should rest on the information the designation process garners. Some of the indirect effects of designation of critical habitat are:

1. The Designation Process Provides Necessary Information for § 10 Permits and Habitat Conservation Plans

Section 10(a) of the ESA (16 U.S.C. § 1539(a)) authorizes the otherwise prohibited taking of listed species if the taking is an incidental part of otherwise lawful activities and if the permit applicant submits a conservation plan (known as a habitat conservation plan or "HCP") that minimizes and mitigates the impacts that likely will result from the taking. Adequate knowledge of the habitat needs of the species in question is crucial to and underlies the process of HCP development and approval and is critical to achieving adequate HCPs. Information on the habitat necessary for the survival and recovery of the species in question and on the relationship of particular properties to the entire area critical for those purposes is crucial. While habitat information can be obtained by the responsible agency aside from the formal process for designation of critical habitat , the designation process is the reviewable means of ensuring that adequate scientific information is in fact obtained and that the habitat needs of the species have been considered simultaneously with a consideration of the economic and other effects of habitat protection.

2. The Designation Process Provides Information for Land Acquisition Decisions

Similarly, the designation of critical habitat process provides information to inform decisions on possible acquisitions of properties for habitat purposes under § 5 of the ESA (16 U.S.C. § 1534).

3. Critical Habitat Informs the Meaning of "Harm" in Definition of "Take"

At the heart of the ESA are its § 9 (16 U.S.C. § 1538) prohibitions against "take" of endangered species. "Take" is defined as killing a listed species, but also includes "harm," which is defined in regulation a including "significant habitat modification or degradation where it actually kills or injures wildlife by significantly impairing essential behavioral patterns, including breeding, feeding or sheltering.[13] Although this definition is not limited to critical habitat, as a practical matter it is easier to demonstrate "significant" habitat modification or degradation if the habitat in question had already been found to be critical to the conservation of the species in question.

4. The Designation Process Informs Development of Recovery Plans

Section 4(f) of the ESA (16 U.S.C. § 1533(f)) requires the preparation of a recovery plan for each listed species. Recovery plans provide guidance on what actions, including habitat maintenance and restoration, are necessary to recover a species. Here again, the designation of critical habitat can play an important role in providing the scientific knowledge of the habitat needs of a species and analysis of effects had impacts that is crucial to development of an effective recovery plan. Any agency habitat studies would be helpful in developing a recovery plan. Any agency habitat studies would be helpful in developing a recovery plan, but the designation process, because it entails specific requirements and is reviewable, arguably provides a sounder basis for recovery plans.

DISCUSSION

The FWS in its notice seeking public comment on the role of habitat in the conservation of endangered species asserts that the only impact of designation is that once an area is designated as critical habitat. Federal agencies are required to consult with the Service to avoid jeopardy, and that critical habitat designation has no regulatory impact when a Federal agency is not involved, whether through funding or a permit or other authorization. Furthermore, the FWS asserts that designation of critical habitat provides little additional protection to most listed

---

[13] 50 C.F.R. § 17.2. This regulation on harm was upheld against a facial challenge in *Babbitt v. Sweet Home Chapter of Communities for a Great Oregon*, 515 U.S. 687 (1995).

species while consuming significant amounts of funding, staff time, and other resources.[14]

These conclusions seem to have resulted from how the FWS has interpreted certain aspects of the ESA. It will be recalled that under the ESA federal agencies must avoid both jeopardy and the destruction or adverse modification of critical habitat. However, the FWS has conflated these two duties by defining "destruction or adverse modification" as meaning "a direct or indirect alteration that appreciably diminishes the value of critical habitat for *both the survival and recovery* of a listed species..."[15] and then interpreting this phrase as essentially meaning "survival," and therefore as being synonymous with jeopardy in most instances.[16] Because it conflated two statutory requirements, the agency then concludes that designation of critical habitat adds nothing that is not already covered by the jeopardy concept. As a result, the FWS has given designation such a low priority that the agency has completed critical habitat designations for only 9% of listed species, [17] substituting instead general agency assertions that agency consideration of habitat needs and effects has been adequate. However, the courts have found that the agency does have a duty to designate critical habitat.[18]

It may be that, while protection of habitat in general is vital to conservation of a species, perhaps the current statutory process for designation of critical habitat may not be the ideal means of accomplishing that end. For example, perhaps the relationship between the gathering of information and consideration of the effects of habitat protection that the critical habitat designation process currently represents and other aspects of the Act (such as the development of HCPs and recovery plans), could be clarified. These issues are presented by S. 1100, in that it proposes moving the decision on designation of critical habitat to the time a

---

[14] *See* 64 Fed. Reg. 31872.

[15] 50 C.F.R. § 402.02. (emphasis added).

[16] *See* 64 Fed. Reg. 31872, which states: "For almost all species, the adverse modification and jeopardy standards are the same..." Whatever Congress may have intended by its directive to avoid destruction or adverse modification of critical habitat, and whatever may be said about the agency's interpretation of its own phrase referring to "both survival and recovery," it is an elementary rule of statutory construction that a statute is to be interpreted to avoid rendering any of its provisions inoperative or superfluous. 2A SUTHERLAND STAT. CONST. §46.06 (5th ed.) (1992 Rev.). *See also,* MICHAEL J. BEAN AND MELANIE J. ROWLAND, THE EVOLUTION OF NATIONAL WILDLIFE LAW 251-261 (3d Ed. 1997), Katherine S, Yagerman, *Protecting Critical Habitat Under the Federal Endangered Species Act,* 20 ENVTL. L. 811 (1990).

[17] The FWS materials accompanying the June 14th notice state that FWS designated critical habitat for 113 of the listed 1,168 species to date.

[18] *See, e. g.,* Conservation Council for Hawaii v. Babbitt, 24 F. Supp. 2d 1074(1078 (D. Hi. 1998), in which the court set deadlines for the FWS to designate critical habitat for a number of species, even if funds were short (a situation plaintiffs alleged FWS was partially responsible for), and that the agency's remedy for its listing duties and funds was Congress.

recovery plan is developed. This may be advisable since accurate knowledge of necessary habitat underlies sound recovery plans, but the change would present questions as to what should be done regarding issuance of §§ 7 and 10 incidental take permits and HCPs in the interim. Should these actions be allowed to go forward during the interim period based only on discretionary agency habitat studies? Or should permit issuance and HCP approvals be expressly linked to preliminary and final designation of critical habitat in accordance with statutory standards and to recovery team recommendations that could also benefit from and rest on the reviewable habitat studies the designation of critical habitat in accordance with statutory standards and to recovery team recommendations that could also benefit from and rest on the reviewable habitat studies the designation process entails? Whatever changes Congress may choose to make, arguably it would remain important to preserve some mandatory, reviewable agency duty to study and reach rational decisions on both habitat needs and the effects of various habitat protection alternatives. These requirements underlie and support other important agency actions affecting both the species in question and landowners, and provide a clear point for judicial review of agency decisions.

Chapter 9

AN ENDANGERED SPECIES ACT ISSUE FOR SOUTHEASTERN FLORIDA: JOHNSON'S SEAGRASS

Eugene H. Buck

ABSTRACT

Johnson's seagrass, a small marine plant growing in shallow estuaries and coastal lagoons only along the Southeastern Florida coast, has been listed by the National Marine Fisheries (NMFS) as a threatened species under the Endangered Species Act (ESA), the first marine plant so listed. The continued existence of this species appears to be most affected by water clarity and sediment disturbance *(e.g.,* stormwater runoff, boating and personal watercraft activities, and siltation) as well as by hurricanes and storm surges. In addition, limited seed production by this species makes its recovery uncertain. State and local government officials, marine industries, and the U.S. Army Corps of Engineers as well as private citizens are concerned that protection under the ESA could preclude, or increase expenses for, routine dredging project and the expansion of three Florida ports. NMFS will seek to protect this species through ESA measures and address local concerns that species protection may interfere with maintenance dredging projects. This report will be updated as this issue evolves.

BACKGROUND

Johnson's seagrass, *Halophila johnsonii*, is a very small (two-inch high) flowering marine plant with the most limited geographic distribution of about 60 species of seagrasses worldwide. It grows on a variety of sediment types ranging from mud to coarse sand discontinuously and patchily[1] in estuaries and coastal lagoons along about 150 miles of the southeastern Florida coast from Sebastian Inlet to Virginia Key in north Biscayne Bay. Although it most frequently grows from the intertidal zone to about six feet below mean tidal height, Johnson's seagrass has been reported growing at depths greater than other seagrass species at 12 feet or deeper in very clear water on tidal deltas adjacent to inlets and in Hobe Sound. As an opportunistic species, Johnson's seagrass expands the total area covered by seagrasses through its ability to survive in environments where other seagrass species cannot—both in the intertidal area above and the subtidal area below other seagrass species. Large patches of their species are reported to occur inside Lake Worth Lagoon, south of West Palm Bach; in Indian River Lagoon, the largest patches are usually on tidal deltas adjacent to inlets.

Johnson's seagrass appears to have a relatively high tolerance for low light levels and fluctuating salinity and temperature—features that may allow this species to colonize environments where other species of seagrass cannot survive. However, severe storms can damage seagrasses through erosion and siltation. During hurricanes, sediments moved by storm surges and other turbulent flow (*e.g.,* waves and currents) can easily dislodge, erode, or bury existing seagrass communities, particularly shallow—rooted species such as Johnson's seagrass. Milder storms can resuspend sediments and limit light penetration.

In general, seagrasses stabilize sediments as well as provide shelter (habitat) and dissolved oxygen for many marine animals. Seagrasses provide micro-habitats for small marine animals and are a source of easily decomposed and digested organic matter (food) for various invertebrates, fish, and larger animals, including endangered West Indian manatees and threatened green sea turtles. Various species of commercially and recreationally valuable fish and shellfish live within seagrass beds. Juvenile fish of various commercially and recreationally important species hide in seagrass beds to escape predators. It is reasonable to infer that a similar ecological role can be attributed to Johnson's seagrass, although study of this species has been limited. In addition, marine biodiversity is greater where Johnson's seagrass occurs.

---

[1] Most patches are less than one square meter in size.

Only female flowers have been observed for Johnson's seagrass, and this species' mechanisms of seed dispersal and establishment of new beds have not been studied. Although some suggest that Johnson's seagrass only reproduces asexually, fruit has been described by several investigators.[2] In addition, this species has a small, shallow rhizome (*i.e.*, root) structure relative to total plant biomass, a high biomass turnover rate, and a rapid lateral spreading rate of as much as 1.25 centimeters per day. The small rhizome structure suggests that Johnson's seagrass is unable to store large energy reserves. While some suggest that these two characteristics—uncertain reproductive capacity and small energy reserves—make Johnson's seagrass vulnerable to stress/disturbance and less likely to repopulate any area from which it disappears, others assert that species with a higher biomass turnover and lateral spreading rates are, in general, better at colonizing available habitat. Johnson's seagrass has been reported in some human-influenced areas of the Intracoastal Waterway, suggesting that this species' ability to repopulate is significant. However, regrowth and reestablishment of surviving populations of Johnson's seagrass could be more difficult than for species with a life history that features a wide dispersal of seeds. The ecology of Johnson's seagrass has not been extensively studied, making generalizations from other species difficult and suspect.

The National Marine Fisheries Service(NMFS) proposed to list Johnson's seagrass as a threatened species on September 15, 1993,[3] and a definition of the critical habitat for this species was proposed on August 4, 1994.[4] On April 20, 1998, NMFS reopened the proposed listing of Johnson's seagrass as a threatened species for additional public comment.[5] On September 14, 1998, NMFS published the final rule listing Johnson's seagrass as a threatened species, effective October 14, 1998.[6] This is the first marine plant listed under the Endangered Species Act (ESA) as a threatened or endangered species. Under the ESA, NMFS is required to consider additional protective regulations for this species.

---

[2] N.J. Eiseman and C. McMillan. "A New Species of Seagrass, *Halophila johnsonii*, from the Atlantic Coast of Florida." *Aquatic Botany*, v. 9 (1980): 15-19; C.J. Dawes, *et al.* "A Comparison of the Physiological Ecology of the Seagrasses *Halophila decipiens* Ostenfeld and *H. johnsonii* Eiseman from Florida." *Aquatic Botany*, v. 33 (1989): 149-154.
[3] 58 *Federal Register* 48326.
[4] 59 *Federal Register* 39716.
[5] 63 *Federal Register* 19468.
[6] 63 *Federal Register* 49035.

HUMAN ACTIVITIES STRESSING THIS SPECIES

Many possible risks for this species are inferred from environmental risks to other species of seagrass. Based on data from other seagrass species and from observations of Johnson's seagrass,[7] continued existence of this species appear to be most affected by reduction of water clarity(*e.g.*, water quality and sediment disturbance, especially from poor stormwater control practices), with additional concerns for boating and personal watercraft activities (propeller scars, anchor mooring, and out-current jet blowouts),[8] dredging of navigation channels, and shading from over-water construction (*e.g.,* docks). The time required for recovery of damaged seagrass ecosystems is affected by a variety of factors, such as the cause and extent of damage, the seagrass species affected, and physical characteristics of the damage site.

Reduction of water clarity caused by human activity and increased coastal land use can threaten seagrass by reducing photosynthesis. Erosion caused by boat wakes may also increase turbidity and siltation. Siltation not only reduces incident light, but can also create anoxic conditions in the sediment by limiting oxygen diffusion. Such anoxic conditions are problematic to seagrasses as they may cause problems with root metabolism or result in the production of compounds, such as sulfides, that can be toxic to the seagrass. With as much as 70% of runoff pollution contributed by non-point sources, water quality problems, especially poor stormwater control practices, can increase water turbidity as well s nutrient loading. Being a deeper water species, Johnson's seagrass is more susceptible to subtle changes in water quality. Excessive nutrients (*e.g.,* nitrogen and phosphorus) from urban and agricultural land runoff can stimulate increased algal growth that severely reduces water clarity and increases epiphyte loading, shading seagrasses. In addition, seagrass habitat may be affected by the timing and duration of stormwater runoff. Although Johnson's seagrass is reported to tolerate a wide range of salinities, additional research is required t better understand this species' ecological response to freshwater inflows.

Propeller scars and anchor mooring can break and excavate seagrass root systems, severing rhizomes, completely removing them from the sediment, and

---

[7] W.J. Kenworthy. *The Distribution, Abundance, and Ecology of* Halophila johnsonii *Eiseman in the Lower Indian River, Florida.* Final Report to the Office of Protected Resources, NMFS. Silver Spring, MD, 1993.

[8] Propeller scars are damage caused to vegetation and bottom habitat by propellers on boat moors operated in shallow water. Anchor mooring refers to damage caused by anchors from boats which can disturb and damage vegetation and bottom habitat, especially if these anchors are dragged along the bottom as boats are pulled by currents. Out-current jets on personal watercraft direct water straight down instead of outward, increasing the potential for sediment "blow-outs."

reducing the physical stability of the community. Severing seagrass rhizomes removes what little stored materials and energy these plant accumulate, making them highly susceptible to any stress, *e.g.*, light limitation due to turbidity. In addition, propellers and anchors often alter bottom topography (*e.g.,* propellers make trenches in the sediment), which influences seagrass recovery time. For example, boats are reported to have damaged or destroyed about 18,000 acres (20%) of the seagrass beds in Biscayne National Park.[9] Personal watercraft (*e.g.,* jet skis) are also recognized as a potential hazard to seagrass beds in very shallow water. Some seagrass beds can require as long as 5 years to recover form minor damage and a decade or more to recover where the wash from a boat motor or personal watercraft operated in shallow water digs a crater in a seagrass bed. However, since seagrass species vary in their ability to recover from scarring, one must be cautious in inferring that such characteristics are also relevant to Johnson's seagrass, which is capable of spreading quickly.[10]

Dredging of navigation channels can resuspend and redistribute sediments, severely decreasing available light, burying plants, and altering bottom topography. However, dredging in Florida is highly regulated to prevent such damage, and Johnson's seagrass continues to occur on tidal deltas adjacent to several inlets that have been regularly dredged for many decades. Major ports, harbors, and navigation channels are maintained at depths greater than 6 feet and Johnson's seagrass has not been reported within such dredged basins or navigation channels—only in adjacent shallow areas. Thus, it would be new dredging in shallow areas, rather than maintenance dredging of previously dredged basins and navigation channels, that would be more likely to affect Johnson's seagrass habitat. Although some have suggested that dredging may have enhanced this species, scientific evidence does not support this argument.

PROTECTION EFFORTS

The state of Florida has taken steps to protect seagrass habitat. New and redeveloped sources of stormwater discharge are required to meet state water management district regulations. Several counties are reportedly installing point-source stormwater management systems that may improve water quality from point sources. In addition, improvements in wastewater treatment within the past two decades are reported to have increased water clarity in Lake Worth and other

---

[9] Associated Press. "Biscayne National Park Scarred by Boat Groundings." August 10, 1998.

[10] If Johnson's seagrass is a weedy species, it might recover more rapidly compared to turtle grass, which has been the subject of most studies on the effects of propeller scarring.

lagoons, allowing seagrass cover to expand. Although limited by federal navigation rules promulgated by the U.S. Coast Guard, state of Florida efforts to mark navigation channels and establish speed zones to protect seagrasses that are adjacent to Florida state parks and are important manatee habitat may promote multiple public benefits.[11] Non-motor and controlled access areas have resulted in improved seagrass habitat.

Since Johnson's seagrass grows on it submerged lands, the state of Florida holds that NMFS measures to protect this species must be consistent with state of Florida policies and involve Florida as a necessary partner. NMFS has an active seagrass program[12] and anticipates proposing separate regulations outlining specific protective measures for this seagrass. Federal activities that may affect Johnson's seagrass and require ESA §7 consultation are identified by NMFS as including Corps of Engineers project authorizations, Environmental Protection Agency discharge permits, Coast Guard vessel traffic regulation, management of refuges and species by the Fish and Wildlife Service, authorization of state coastal zone management plans by the National Ocean Service, and commercial fishery management by NMFS. NMFS anticipated reopening the public comment period on the proposed designation of critical habitat before making a final decision on whether and, if so, where to designate such critical habitat. The state of Florida questions whether the best available scientific data as well as socio-economic evaluations support the proposed critical habitat.[13] Protecting Johnson's seagrass habitat would also afford additional protection for the six other seagrass species found in Florida waters as well as to the animal communities that depend on these plants.

CONTROVERSY

Some characterize the concern over Johnson's seagrass as being a traditional conflict between environmental preservation and economic development. Although NMFS anticipates maintenance dredging can be authorized through ESA §7 consultations for areas where Johnson's seagrass occurs, some

---

[11] Frank J. Sargent, *et al. Scarring of Florida's Seagrasses: Assessment and Management Options.* FMRI Technical Report TR-1. St. Petersburg, FL: Florida Department of Environmental Protection, Florida Marine Research Institute, 1995. 43 p.

[12] Mark S. Fonseca, *et al. Guidelines for the Conservation and Restoration of Seagrasses in the United States and Adjacent Waters.* NOAA Coastal Ocean Program Decision Analysis Series No. 12. Silver Spring, MD: NOAA Coastal Ocean Office, November 1998. 22 p.

[13] For example, the state claims that most Johnson's seagrass meadows have been found within Lake Worth Lagoon, rather than within the inlet areas previously proposed for designation.

individuals are concerned that protection under the ESA could preclude, or increase the expense for, routine dredging projects and the expansion of three southeast Florida ports. More specifically, Martin Country public services executives are concerned that listing of Johnson's seagrass could jeopardize future plans to reconfigure St. Lucie Inlet to retard beach erosion.[14] Additional measures required to protect Johnson's seagrass at dredging projects may include more detailed site surveys and reduced mixing zones for dredge-generated turbidity—measures unlikely to significantly increase overall project costs.[15] In addition, NMFS may issue and ESA permit for "taking" or displacing one or several Johnson's seagrass populations in St. Lucie Inlet if this limited dredging project is determined unlikely to jeopardize the continued existence of the species.

Although Johnson's seagrass is uncommon in the Intracoastal Waterway, some are concerned that its presence could impede routine maintenance dredging in the limited segments of this transportation corridor where it does occur. However, NMFS has concluded an ESA §7 consultation with the Corps of Engineers on maintenance dredging of existing, authorized federal navigation projects in this area, and determined that maintenance dredging of those channels constructed within the last 10 years is unlikely to jeopardize the continued existence of Johnson's seagrass.

The Florida Department of Environmental Protection has expressed concern to NMFS that information on this species is inadequate for deciding on appropriate protection and recovery efforts, and has suggested that NMFS consider a focused, protection-oriented research effort on Johnson's seagrass to assure that the most appropriate management strategies for the species can be developed to reconcile development with species protection. Until Johnson's seagrass and its ecology are better understood, scientists suggest protecting this species by taking a cautious and conservative approach to dealing with problems affecting it and its habitat.[16]

---

[14] Edward Filo. "Protected Sea Grass Threatens Inlet Plans." *Vero Beach Press-Journal,* October 6, 1998.

[15] Personal communication with Keith Mille, Environmental Specialist, Florida Department of Environmental Protection, Tallahassee, on October 30, 1998.

[16] Personal communication with dr. Richard L. Turner, Associate Professor, Florida Institute of Technology, Melbourne, on October 23, 1998.

Chapter 10

PACIFIC SALMON AND ANADROMOUS TROUT: MANAGEMENT UNDER THE ENDANGERED SPECIES ACT

John R. Dandelski

ABSTRACT

Along the Pacific Coast, 26 distance population segments of Pacific salmon and steelhead trout are listed as either endangered or threatened under the Endangered Species Act (ESA). A variety of human activities have combined to greatly reduce or eliminate historic fish habitat, degrade remaining habitat, and otherwise harm populations of anadromous (sea-run) fish. In addition, natural phenomena stress fish populations and contribute to their variable abundance. Current management efforts aim to restore the abundance of ESA-listed native northeast Pacific salmonids to historic, sustainable population levels. This report summarizes the reasons for ESA listings and outlines efforts to protect ESA-listed species. This report will be updated periodically to reflect the changing situation.

BACKGROUND

Pacific chinook, coho, chum, sockeye, and pink salmon as well as steelhead trout are and anadromous, *i.e.,* they live as juveniles in fresh water, migrate to the ocean to develop, and, when sexually mature, return to freshwater to spawn. While steelhead trout and Atlantic salmon can return to the sea after Spawn again in subsequent years, Pacific salmon die after spawning once. Juvenile salmon typically reside in fresh water from a few days (pink salmon) to 3 years (some sockeye salmon) before migrating to the ocean, where they typically spend 1-6 years before migrating back to their natal stream, as much as 900 miles or more inland. Natural phenomena—predators, droughts, floods, and fluctuating oceanic conditions—stress salmonids and contribute to the variable abundance of their populations. *El Niño* conditions have been of particular concern with warmer marine waters reducing food organisms for salmonids and bringing an abundance of predators, such as mackerel.

By the late 1990s, west coast salmon abundance had declined to only 10-15% of what it had been in the 1800s.[1] Precipitous salmon declines in the 1990s hurt the economies of fishing-dependent coastal and rural inland communities throughout the Northwest and northern California. As recently as 1988, sport and commercial salmon fishing in that region generated more than $1.25 billion for the regional economy. Since then, salmon fishing closures have contributed to the loss of nearly 80% of this region's job base, with a total salmon industry loss over the past 30 years of approximately 72,000 family wage jobs.[2]

As of early April 2001, 26 distinct population segments of five salmonid species had been listed as either endangered or threatened under the Endangered Species Act (ESA, see table 1).[3] While no *species* of anadromous trout or salmon is in danger of near-term extinction, individual population segments (designated as "evolutionarily significant units")[4] within these species have declined substantially or have even been extirpated. The American Fisheries Society considers at least 214 Pacific Coast anadromous fish populations to be "at risk" while at least 106 other historically abundant populations have already become extinct.[5]

---

[1] E. Winninghoff. "Where Have All the Salmon Gone?" *Forbes* (Nov. 21, 1994): 104-116.
[2] Pacific Rivers Council. The Economic Imperative of Protecting Riverine Habitat in the Pacific Northwest. Eugene, OR: January 1992; and "Statement of Glen Spain of the Pacific Coast Federation of Fishermen's Associations" in: U.S. Senate, Committee on Environment and Public Works, Subcommittee on Drinking Water, Fisheries, and Wildlife. *Endangered Species Act Reauthorization*. Hearing, June 1, 1995. Roseburg, OR: U.S. Govt. Print Off. Pp. 123-142.
[3] Table information taken from: U.S. Dept. of Commerce, National Marine Fisheries Service, "Listing Status Snapshot" ([http://WWW.NWR.NOAA.GOV/1salmon/salmesa/index.htm], updated March 29, 2001.)
[4] NMFS uses the term "evolutionarily significant unit" (ESU) as synonymous to a distinct population segment that appears to be reproductively isolated from other segments (56 *Federal Register*58612, November 20, 1991).
[5] Willa Nehlsen, Jack Williams, and James Lichatowich. "Pacific Salmon at the Crossroads: Stocks at Risk from California, Oregon, Idaho, and Washington." *Fisheries*, v. 16 (1991):4-21; and T.L. Slaney, et al. "Status of Anadromous Salmon and Trout in British Columbia and Yukon." *Fisheries*, v. 21 (October 1996): 20-35.

HUMAN ACTIVITIES STRESSING FISH

Anadromous salmonids inhibit clean, silt-free streams of low water temperature (below 68°F) and quality estuarine nursery habitat. Human activities—logging, grazing, mining, agriculture, urban development, and consumptive water use—can degrade aquatic habitat. Silt can cover streambed gravel, smothering eggs. Poorly constructed roads often increase siltation in streams where adult salmon spawn and young salmon rear. Removal of streamside trees and shade frequently leads to higher water temperatures. Grazing cattle remove streamside vegetation and exacerbate streambank erosion. Urbanization typically brings riprap channelization and filled wetlands, altering food supplies and nursery habitat. Habitat alterations can lead to increased salmonid predation by marine mammals, birds, and other fish. Water diversions for agriculture exacerbate these problems. In the Klamath River basin, as much as 90% of the annual flow from the Trinity River was diverted to California's Central Valley Project for irrigation. According to state water resource agencies, almost every water basis in Oregon, eastern Washington, and northern California is now over-appropriated (*i.e.,* there are more legal permits for diversion than available water) during the hottest and driest months of the year.

Dams for hydropower, flood control, and irrigation substantially alter aquatic habitat and can have significant impacts n anadromous fish. While the design of some dams is described as "fish-friendly" (*e.g.,* Wells Dam on the Columbia River in Washington), poorly designed dams can physically bar or impede anadromous fish migrations to and from the sea, kill juveniles as they pass through a dam's turbines, and expose fish to potentially harmful gas supersaturation.[6] If delayed by days during migration, both young and old salmon can be exposed to increased predation, to an increased risk of bacterial infections, and to higher temperatures which cause stress and sometimes death.[7] Decreased river flow can also harm juveniles by delaying their downstream migration. However, the eight federally owned mainstem dams in the Columbia River basin produce about two-thirds of the power in the Pacific Northwest,[8] and the reservoirs behind these dams create a major navigable waterway as far inland as Lewiston, Idaho.

---

[6] Water spilled from dams can become supersaturated with gaseous nitrogen. Juvenile fish exposed to supersaturated conditions can develop disorienting gas bubble disease and become more susceptible to predation.
[7] G. F. Cada, *et al.* "Effects of Water Velocity on the Survival of Downstream-Migrating Juvenile Salmon and Steelhead: A Review with Emphasis on the Columbia River Basin." *Reviews in Fisheries Science,* v. 5, no. 2 (1997): 131-183.

The goal of fish hatcheries, operated along the Pacific Coast since 1877, was, and continues to be, the augmentation of natural salmonid populations and the production of fish to replace those lost where dams completely blocked passage and destroyed native salmonid populations. Today, at least 80% of the salmon caught commercially in the Pacific Northwest and northern California each year come from hatcheries. In the 1970s, however, scientists discovered that some hatchery and transplantation has generally resulted in decreased genetic fitness of wild populations and the loss of some stream-specific adaptations. Also, hatchery fish generally have lower survival rates than wild fish, and are less able to adjust to changing ocean conditions or to escape predators.

The harvest of intermingled fish populations from different watershed presents several problems, including how to protect ESA-listed populations while promoting the harvest of abundant native and hatchery fish. Since hatcheries are often more productive than natural fish populations, managing fisheries to avoid surplus returns to hatcheries can result in over harvested natural populations. Controversy arises when managers must consider how much the harvest of abundant populations must be curtailed to protect less-abundant ESA-listed populations. Such policies can frustrate both commercial fishermen and sport anglers. ESA-listed or seriously depressed populations thus can become the limiting factor on fisheries, resulting in tens of millions of dollars in foregone fishing opportunities to avoid further depressing the weakest populations.

PROTECTION AND RESTORATION EFFORTS

The task of implementing the ESA for anadromous salmonids falls to the National Marine Fisheries Service (NMFS) in the Department of Commerce. NMFS can receive a petition or initiate the process to determine whether a species or population merits listing as either "endangered" or "threatened." Based on facts presented in the petition, the Secretary of Commerce decides whether the petition present substantial information indicating that listing may be warranted. If the Secretary decides that the petitioned action may be warranted, a 90-day notice announcing the initiation of a status review is published in the *Federal Register.* Once the status review is completed, NMFS publishes a notice of proposed rulemaking in the *Federal Register* and seeks public comment for those species or populations NMFS believes should be listed. A final listing decision must occur within 12 months after notice publication. Once listed, NMFS is required to

---

[8] "Saving the Columbia Salmon," *Seattle Times* (June 8, 1997): B4-B6.

designate critical habitat[10] as well as develop and publish a recovery plan for the species. The goal of ESA listing is species recovery, defined as removal from the ESA list. NMFS is in the early stages of a long process aimed at recovering ESA-listed salmonid ESUs as well as avoiding future listings.

When a federal activity may harm an ESA-listed species, the ESA requires the federal agency to consult with NMFS to determine whether the activity is likely to jeopardize the survival and recovery of the species or adversely modify its critical habitat. In response to a biological assessment submitted by the federal agency, NMFS issues a "biological opinion" (BO) with an incidental "take" statement which can authorize a limited take of the species and specifies reasonable and prudent measures to minimize such taking of the species. If NMFS issues a jeopardy opinion, it includes a reasonable and prudent alternative which would be expected to jeopardize the continued existence of the species. NMFS issues numerous BOs related to salmon each year. For example, a 1995 BO for the U.S. Army Corps of Engineers and the Bonneville Power Administration sought to develop a biologically sound strategy to deal with salmon passage in the Columbia and Snake Rivers. The major impact of this 1995 BO and its 1998 supplement has been the move away from transporting the majority of juvenile salmonids downstream by truck or barge, and implementing a "spread the risk" policy which calls for an increase in spilling water and fish over dams, thus circumventing the power-producing turbines, to speed juvenile fish through the river toward the ocean with lower mortality. In 2000, the Corps completed a System Operations Review of the Columbia and Snake River hydropower system, with breaching the four lower Snake River dams being considered as one option. In December 2000, NMFS issued a revised BO that reviewed the strategies outlined in the 1995 and 1998 BOs and recommend changes.[11] This BO did not recommend breaching the four Lower Snake River dams.

Prior to the listing of salmonid ESUs under the ESA, the majority of salmon conservation efforts were conducted by individual states, tribes, and private industries that managed salmon habitat. In the Columbia River Basin, the Northwest Power Planning Council took the lead under the 1980 Pacific Northwest Electric Power Planning and Conservation Act (P.L. 96-501), by attempting to protect salmon and their habitat while also providing economical power to the region. Subsequently, federal agencies and public utilities spent hundreds of millions of dollars on technical improvements for dams, habitat

---

[10] There may be no critical habitat designation, if NMFS decides that it is nor prudent, and the critical habitat designation may be delayed up to a year if it is not determinable. In practice, only about 20% of listed species have designated critical habitat.

[11] See BO text at [http://www.nwr.noaa.gov/1hydrop/hydroweb/docs/Final/2000Biop.html].

enhancement, and water purchases to improve salmon survival, yet many populations have continued to decline. Recent years have seen an increased interest by state governments and tribal councils in developing comprehensive salmon management efforts. States generally seek to prevent ESA listings, or, if listings do occur, to reduce federal involvement affecting state-managed lands. With limited staff and funding to implement a wide range of programs, NMFS has encouraged integrated management efforts (*i.e.,* habitat conservation plans) among federal, state, and tribal agencies as a powerful and necessary tool in saving listed salmonid species, as well as possibly avoiding the need for future listing of additional ESUs through state-managed comprehensive recovery efforts.[12] NMFS viewed the Oregon Coastal Salmon Restoration Initiative (OCSRI), to promote comprehensive and proactive state-based recovery efforts and avoid listing coho salmon in Oregon, as precedent for federal/state/local partnerships. However, a federal court decision clarified that, to avoid an eventual listing, such plans cannot be based primarily on speculative or proposed future measures, but must instead be based on recovery measures that are enforceable or reasonably likely to occur, as, for instance, measures embodies in laws, regulations, or long-range and stable funding mechanisms.[13] With the listing of many salmonid ESUs in the Columbia River basin, management has become increasingly constrained, and new options for governance are being explored by federal, state, and tribal parties. Restoration efforts for some California salmon, including water reforms, were embodied in the Central Valley Project Improvement Act (Title XXXIV of P.L. 102-575). The U.S. Fish and Wildlife Service has been coordinating plans for fish screens, fish ladders and water pollution reduction, to double by 2002 the native fish populations in the Central Valley Project area.

NMFS has issued an interim policy on artificial propagation of Pacific salmon under the ESA to provide guidance on how hatcheries should be used to help recover salmonids.[14] In general, the policy is to recover wild populations in their natural habitat wherever possible, without resorting to artificial propagation. Washington, Oregon, and wherever possible, without resorting to artificial propagation. Washington, Oregon, and British Columbia have instituted programs to mark hatchery coho salmon by fin clipping so that marked fish can be readily identified by fishermen as hatchery fish and selectively retained at harvest while unmarked, native fish can be released to spawn. Similar programs are underway

---

[12] Personal communication with Garth Griffin, Branch Chief, Protected Resources Division, NMFS, Portland, OR, on May 21, 1998.
[13] Oregon Natural Resources Council v. Daley, CV-97-1155-ST (D. Or. June 1, 1998).
[14] 58 *Federal Register* 17573, Apr. 5, 1993.

for other species, such as Chinook salmon and steelhead trout. In addition, controversy and resistance remain over suggested changes to using fishing gear more suitable to releasing wild fish unharmed after being caught inadvertently. The bilateral 1985 Pacific Salmon Treaty regulates the harvest of salmon of U.S. and Canadian origin. While the Treaty calls for reducing interception of the other country's fish, it also calls on the parties to avoid undue disruption of existing fisheries. However, ESA protective measures, including the prohibition against taking ESA-listed fish and the designation of critical habitat, could be undercut by U.S. and Canadian fishermen catching ESA-listed fish as they migrate through Alaskan and Canadian waters.

Table 1: Status of Six Species of Pacific Coast Salmonids

Species	Population (ESU)	Status (E-Endangered T-Threatened)	FR Citation	Pending Actions
Coho salmon (*Oncorhynchus kisutch*)	1. Central California	Threatened	1. 61 FR 56138 Oct. 31, 1996	
	2. Southern Oregon/Northern CA coast	Threatened	2. 62 FR 24588 May 6, 1997	
	3. Oregon Coast	Threatened	3. 63 FT 42587 Aug. 10, 1998	
	4. Puget Sound/Strait of Georgia	Candidate	4. 60 FR 38001 July 25, 1995	Complete listing assessments for candidate ESUs
	5. Southwest WA/Lower Columbia River	Candidate	5. 60 FR 38001 July 25, 1995	
Chinook salmon (*Oncorhynchus tshawytscha*)	1. Sacramento River winter-run	Endangered	1. FR 12832 Apr. 6, 1990 55 FR 49623 Nov. 30, 1990 59 FR 13836 Mar. 23, 1994	Develop proposed 4(d) rules for Central Valley spring-run and California coastal ESUs
	2. Snake River fall-run	Threatened	2. 57 FR 14653 Apr. 22, 1992	
	3. Snake River spring/summer-run	Threatened	3. 57 FR 14653 Apr. 22, 1992	
	4. Central Valley spring-run.	Threatened	4. 64 FR 50393 Sept. 16, 1999	
	5. Upper Columbia River spring-run	Endangered	5. 64 FR 14308 Mar. 24, 1999	
	6. California coastal	Threatened	6. 64 FR 50393 Sept. 16, 1999	
	7. Puget Sound	Threatened	7. 64 FR 14308 Mar. 24, 1999	
	8. Lower Columbia River	Threatened	8. 64 FR 14308 Mar. 24, 1999	
	9. Upper Willamette River	Threatened	9. 64 FR 14308 Mar. 24, 1999	
	10. Central Valley fall and late-fall run	Candidate	10. 64 FR 50393 Sept. 16, 1999	Complete listing assessments for candidate ESU

Species		Location	Status	Reference	Notes
Chum salmon (*Oncorhynchus keta*)	1.	Hood Canal summer-run	Threatened	1. 64 FR 14508 Mar. 25, 1999	
	2.	Columbia River	Threatened	2. 64 FR 14508 Mar. 25, 1999	
Sockeye salmon (*Oncorhynchus nerka*)	1.	Snake River	Endangered	1. 64 FR 14508 Mar. 25, 1999	
	2.	Ozette River	Threatened	2. 64 FR 14508 Mar. 25, 1999	
	1.	Southern California	Endangered	1. 62 FR 43937 Aug. 18, 1997	
	2.	South-Central California Coast	Threatened	2. 62 FR 43937 Aug. 18, 1997	
	3.	Central California Coast	Threatened	3. 62 FR 43937 Aug. 18, 1997	
	4.	Upper Columbia River	Endangered	4. 62 FR 43937 Aug. 18, 1997	
	5.	Snake River Basin	Threatened	5. 63 FR 43937 Aug. 18, 1997	
Steelhead trout (*Oncorhynchus mykess*)	6.	Lower Columbia River	Threatened	6. 63 FR 13347 Mar. 19, 1998	
	7.	California Central Valley	Threatened	7. 63 FR 13347 Mar. 19, 1998	
	8.	Upper Willamette River	Threatened	8. 64 FR 14517 Mar. 25, 1999	Develop 4(d) rule for northern
	9.	Middle Columbia River	Threatened	9. 64 FR 14517 Mar. 25, 1999	California ESU
	10.	Northern California	Threatened	10. 65 FR 36074 June 7, 2000	Complete listing
	11.	Oregon Coast	Candidate	11. 63 FR 13347 Mar. 19, 1998	assessments for candidate ESU
Sea-run cutthroat Trout (*Oncorhunchus clarki clarki*)	1.	Southwest Washington/Columbia River	Proposed (T)	1. 64 FR 16397 Apr. 5, 1999	Note this species is now under the
	2.	Oregon Coast	Candidate	2. 64 FR 16397 Apr. 5, 1999	jurisdiction of the U.S. Fish and Wildlife Service

INDEX